Lessons Learned from the Special Education Classroom

Lessons Learned from the Special Education Classroom

Creating Opportunities for All Students to Listen, Learn, and Lead

Peg Grafwallner

ROWMAN & LITTLEFIELD
Lanham • Boulder • New York • London

Published by Rowman & Littlefield
An imprint of The Rowman & Littlefield Publishing Group, Inc.
4501 Forbes Boulevard, Suite 200, Lanham, Maryland 20706
www.rowman.com

Unit A, Whitacre Mews, 26-34 Stannary Street, London SE11 4AB

Copyright © 2018 by Peggy J. Grafwallner

All rights reserved. No part of this book may be reproduced in any form or by any electronic or mechanical means, including information storage and retrieval systems, without written permission from the publisher, except by a reviewer who may quote passages in a review.

British Library Cataloguing in Publication Information Available

Library of Congress Cataloging-in-Publication Data

Name: Grafwallner, Peggy J., 1960–, author.
Title: Lessons learned from the special education classroom : creating opportunities for all students to listen, learn, and lead / Peggy J. Grafwallner.
Description: Lanham, Maryland : Rowman & Littlefield, [2018] | Includes bibliographical references.
Identifiers: LCCN 2018026461 (print) | LCCN 2018048076 (ebook) | ISBN 9781475844276 (electronic) | ISBN 9781475844252 (cloth : alk. paper) | ISBN 9781475844269 (pbk. : alk. paper)
Subjects: LCSH: Special education. | Children with disabilities—Education. | Classroom management. | Teacher effectiveness.
Classification: LCC LC3965 (ebook) | LCC LC3965 .G74 2018 (print) | DDC 371.9—dc23
LC record available at https://lccn.loc.gov/2018026461

∞ ™ The paper used in this publication meets the minimum requirements of American National Standard for Information Sciences Permanence of Paper for Printed Library Materials, ANSI/NISO Z39.48-1992.

Printed in the United States of America

To my mom, Jean, who loved to write,

To my brother, Jim, who loved to read,

To my husband, Mike, who learned to listen,

To my son, Max, who is my best work,

and

To my daughter, Ani, who inspires us all.

Contents

Foreword ... ix
    Dave Stuart Jr.

Acknowledgments ... xi

1. Accept Every Student as They Are ... 1
2. Scaffolding a Lesson Is Just Good Teaching ... 11
3. Responding to Every Student ... 23
4. Students Want to Feel Loved ... 33
5. Empathy, Equality, and Equity ... 41
6. The Community of Family ... 51
7. Change Your Language, Change Your Mind-set ... 65
8. Share What You've Learned with Others ... 75
9. Ask Your Colleagues for Help ... 83
10. Celebrate—It's Good for the Soul ... 93

References ... 97

About the Author ... 101

Foreword

Dave Stuart Jr.

I first began corresponding with Peg several years ago. From the start, I was impressed by the mind and heart that she brought to her work, in both her classroom and her writing. After reading the articles she's written for *Edutopia*, I started rooting for her to write a book, so that we all might hold in our hands a collection of her thoughts and insights into our work in the classroom. When I met her during a workshop tour in Wisconsin, I grew impatient with waiting—I wanted to see that book! And so it was with much delight, then, that I first opened the manuscript for this book you're holding now.

In *Lessons Learned from the Special Education Classroom: Creating Opportunities for All Students to Listen, Learn, and Lead*, Peg has given us a resource to guide us through challenges all classroom teachers experience. How do we break down lessons for all students? How do we avoid categorizing kids by their labels and instead give them room to be accepted as they are? How do we manage classrooms instead of punitively removing kids from the learning environment? How can we use language to shape the mindsets of us teachers, as well as those of our students? And on and on. In this book, Peg gives us all kinds of things to think about and ways to improve our craft. We walk away from its pages with new approaches, clear strategies, and things to think on further.

Peg's decades of teaching and coaching are clear on every page of this book. When she gives us ideas for teacher–parent communication, she shares both what has worked for her and what hasn't. In sections like these, I find my own knowledge of the craft getting sometimes challenged—in good ways—and other times reaffirmed. This is just what I want in a professional reading book—something that calls me into engagement.

In my interactions with educators around the country, I can say with confidence that we need all the encouragement and tools we can get. This is a hard time for educators in the United States, but there's perhaps been no greater opportunity to advance the long-term flourishing of students *and* teachers before. What we need are more teachers like Peg: earnestly engaged in the craft, asking the hard questions, looking for the kinds of solutions that a teacher can carry out for not just a few months but for a career. And that is why I think you'll enjoy and benefit from this book—because it's made by an educator and a practitioner who's been immersed in the work all these years.

Acknowledgments

To my new friend and best editor in the whole wide world, Sarah Jubar, a mere thank-you sounds woefully inadequate, but here goes: Sarah, thank you for all you have done for me. I still can't believe we are here. You have made this process so doable and enjoyable. I have loved every minute of the writing process and stretching myself to fulfill my dream of being an author. Thank you for your quick replies, your common sense, and your honest feedback. I could not have done this without you.

April Nagel, you were the inspiration behind the original *Edutopia* article "What I've Learned from Special Ed Teachers." Ani's and my dealings with special education, and unfortunately most of Ani's teachers, were a disaster when she was in school. We often felt unheard and marginalized. However, my attitude toward special education changed when I met you and saw the work you did with students. You made it look effortless, you loved every student, you reached out to all parents *and* you adhered to district policy. Oh, how I wish my Ani had had a teacher like you.

To my "academic family" at Ronald Reagan IB High School, I am forever grateful to all of you who have welcomed me into your classrooms—listening, learning, and leading. I am a better educator and a better person because of all of you. There is no doubt that the best, most caring, and most professional educational staff is at RRHS!

A special shout-out to Suzanne Milewski, my webmaster. You created a professional, user-friendly website that attracts bloggers, readers, and publishers. Thank you for making me look so good!

To my dear friend and inspirational writing muse, Robert Ward. I shared my writing dream with you, and you helped make it happen. I have learned so much from you. Thank you! Your blog (https://rewardingeducation.wordpress.com/) is an inspiration to so many educators. XXOO.

Finally, I would be remiss if I just didn't name those who are as excited about my book as I am—you know who you are: Debbie, Mary, Jerry, Sherry, Judy, Joyce, Teri, Cindy, and Alisa. Thank you!

Finally, I have loved every minute of writing, editing, and growing. I could ask for no better way to spend my life. It truly is a wonderful life.

Chapter One

Accept Every Student as They Are

Students come to us with packages and baggage. It is important to open and unpack each student's background slowly and gently, with kindness, respect, and understanding. Building a relationship with a student takes time and patience; allow it to happen organically. If you force it, you'll have to start all over, and the relationship may or may not bloom.

Academically, students typically fall into three categories: special education, average, and gifted and talented. Interestingly, education has made sure to label each category for ease of use.

SPECIAL EDUCATION

Special education students, while protected by law, are a vulnerable population. Often, parents are thankful for the assistance they have been given by the school district, not realizing they could be entitled to more. Trying to navigate through special education acronyms and laws can be difficult.

As the classroom teacher, remember that the parent who sits in front of you wants to be an academic partner with you for the sake of her child. Therefore, try to gather as much information as possible from the parent to create the very best learning situation for her child. Because you may not know the academic background of the student or the special education journey that the parent has experienced, keep in mind that there may have been difficulty in getting services or support for her child. Try to see the situation from the parent's perspective.

The following are some parent tips to assist the classroom teacher in creating that academic partnership:

Never accept "no." Therapists, case workers, doctors, psychiatrists, principals, teachers, family, friends, and neighbors have told the parent "no." No, she can't play the game because the directions are too hard. No, he can't play baseball because of his emotional outbursts. No, she'll never live on her own. Special education parents have heard "no" all their lives. Be the teacher who says "yes."

Network. Other families are going through very similar experiences. Can you create a network of parents to share experiences and resources? How about a newsletter of resources? Help parents find places of acceptance—like a festival or holiday party that caters to a special needs population. In networking, parents can find solace in other families' stories, and many parents might find peace within their own stories. Help them to create opportunities where there might otherwise be none.

Encourage parents to accept the label. The label "special needs" might be difficult for some families to accept. Many parents' expectations might not be aligned with their children's reality, or they may not know where to go or whom to talk to about their children's diagnoses. Talking with the school social worker or the district special needs director and other parents might help them to embrace the label and realize how it could benefit their children (opportunities for recreational outings, social-emotional role-play, and job coaching support, to name just a few).

Encourage a break. At some point, parents need a break. You might see a concerned child, or you might receive a phone call from a harried parent. All of us, especially parents of special needs children, need the opportunity to unwind. Suggest an afternoon with a friend or an hour of quiet time. Parents may not realize that they need a little time to call their own. Encourage them to take it slowly—but take it.

Know your limitations. It is easy to become mired in the challenges associated with a special needs student. We want to help all our students, especially those who seem to need us a little more. But be aware of your own limitations. It is easy to become the second, third, or fourth partner in a family relationship—one who offers the educational background for a special needs student even after the final bell of the day has rung. Be the teacher who can assist and support; that is all a family wants or needs.

Help parents find their children's gifts. The educational barriers to overcome might seem especially daunting to parents. Find students' areas of strength and celebrate them with their parents. Our special needs students can learn and want to learn. Help parents find their children's awesome gifts. Record a laugh. Share a painting. Take a picture of cooperation. Parents might not be able to see the gifts every day; help them to discover them.

Never stop learning. Be the role model of academic and behavioral learning. Share with parents the classes, courses, or workshops you are taking on autism awareness, cognitively impaired instruction, or mindfulness training. Perhaps you could offer a workshop during an open house, showcasing a particular strategy you recently learned. Let parents know you are bringing what you've learned to the classroom to benefit all students. Share your information with parents; perhaps some of them may be interested in attending these opportunities, too.

Be careful of "experts." Every parent has met an expert or a person who thinks he or she is an expert. In the beginning of their children's academic journeys, most parents trust everyone they meet. However, after time, some parents might have grown jaded. Be aware of your language to parents (i.e., don't call yourself an expert), and don't promise what you can't deliver. Here are suggestions to help parents find a *true* expert in the field:

- Encourage parents to vet the expert online and with other parents.
- Persuade parents to be in the room when the expert is working with their children.
- Encourage parents to ask questions as the expert is working with their children.
- Tell parents that, if their gut is telling them to walk away, then do it. They're probably right.

Be a promoter of your special needs students. Give your special education students every possible opportunity. Hold a talent show that showcases all students' gifts—not just those with singing careers already forged. Manage a café run by your special needs students selling snacks and beverages. Co-coach a Special Olympics event held at your school. Initiate a Best Buddies chapter at your school to connect regular education students with a special needs buddy. Put your students out there to show the world that all students can contribute and all students are unique.

Laugh and cry. Give yourself the space and time to laugh. You will have great moments with all of your students. Enjoy them. Revel in them. Likewise, give yourself the space and time to cry. You deserve it. You've earned it. Take it.

THE GRAY-AREA STUDENTS

Our brightest students are labeled "gifted and talented" and are often steered toward rigorous AP and IB courses. They are encouraged to join such clubs as Odyssey of the Mind or Mensa for Kids. They are embraced by a society that loves winners.

On the other hand, our special education population is protected by law through an individualized education plan (IEP) designed specifically for each student. They are given certain designations that allow them more time on some tests or exemptions from others. They are pulled from classes for small-group direct instruction. They are allowed certain opportunities that other students are not.

But what about the children in the middle—the average, gray-area students? These students have not earned GPAs that are proudly displayed in school hallways, but they do not have special education teachers to scaffold the classroom lecture. What happens to *them*? They sit in their seats, keep quiet, and produce work that is average. Their parents are grateful they do not receive negative academic phone calls, and their teachers are grateful they are not part of the "student fail" list.

Society might believe average is satisfactory—until one reads the synonyms for *average*: *typical, mediocre, ordinary, normal,* and *unexceptional*. Try telling a parent that his child is unexceptional. Yet every time the word *average* is used, that is really what is being said. Therefore, *average* can no longer be an accepted adjective. Teachers cannot and should not tolerate average as the norm.

Many parents of gray-area students are not sure how to advocate for their children. They may not have the language to begin the process. They are the silent parents who accept the way their children's education has been instead of the way their children's education should be. To that end, you can guide them in advocating for their children.

The following are some suggestions for how teachers and parents can work as a team to assist gray-area students in becoming classroom leaders:

Begin by changing your vocabulary. Stop using the words *struggling* or *reluctant* to describe a student (e.g., *struggling reader* or *reluctant reader*); instead, use *developing*, which explains that the student is just not there—yet.

Eliminate the word *average* from your lexicon. Use specific words to assist parents in understanding where their children need support. Think about using these words to clarify your meaning: *ambitious, assured, astute, careful, commend, contentious, determined, diligent, effort, encourage, guidance, insightful, inspire, methodical, observant, open-minded, practical, puzzled, striving, systematic,* and *understanding.* Also, use clarifying phrases to be as unambiguous as you can. In changing language, all students are supported—not just those who seem to get it every time:

- Let me explain that in more detail.
- Let me put it another way.
- In other words, _____.
- To say this differently, _____.

Have a Get-to-Know-Your-Teacher Lunch. Ask students to join you for lunch in your classroom, where you can learn more about them, away from the classroom expectations. Have lunch with a small group—perhaps two or three at a time. You can learn student interests and pursuits in the hopes of enhancing the lesson plan and creating a classroom community.

Encourage students to take advantage of after-school tutoring, peer-review opportunities, or peer study groups. If possible, ask upperclassmen and -women to come to your classroom before school, during lunch, or after school to offer academic help.

Encourage parents to network with other parents by joining the PTA or volunteering in the office. This interaction will give parents the opportunity to learn how other parents request support for their children—or it might give them a chance to meet with the principal and advocate for their children and others.

Encourage parents to attend school-based functions with their children. Suggest the parent and her child go to the art fair, the world languages program, the musicals. In this way, parents show support of the school programs, and hopefully, their children will see the value of being an integral part of the school community.

Create postcards that highlight student positives or showcase student problem solving. Postcards can be sent out to parents every few weeks highlighting a positive assessment, sharing a particularly difficult problem-solving technique, or showcasing a meaningful student discussion.

Encourage students to seek out opportunities for growth, such as clubs, activities, athletics, and positive peers. Students might not know all of the opportunities available to them, especially in a large middle school or high school. Schedule a club day in your classroom, where representatives from various clubs, activities, or athletics can share information.

GIFTED AND TALENTED

It is not unusual for gifted and talented students to seamlessly float through elementary, middle, and high school. However, while it may look effortless, teachers and parents know the time and work these students dedicate to being their best academic selves.

Gifted and talented students are often overlooked because it is assumed they will learn in spite of the classroom teacher. Even if the teacher is not necessarily a solid educator, these students will still learn and make gains. But this isn't good enough. Parents and students must demand educators who are able to design, implement, and assess vigorous learning opportunities for all students—especially those who are considered high performing. The following suggestions help build collaborative relationships with parents and develop learning alternatives.

Make sure you know the definition of *gifted and talented*. How is *gifted and talented* defined in your state? Check the department of public instruction website for the most recent definition. Often, the words have multiple meanings, and teachers and parents are quick to throw around the terms *high performing*, *leadership capability*, and *appropriate education*. Know what *gifted and talented* entails so you can be the best advocate for your students and their parents.

If you believe one of your students is gifted and talented, request to have her tested by the school psychologist. The data will support you in advocating for her. If the child qualifies as gifted and talented (and even if she does not), design productive work meant to mirror the student's abilities. According to Brasher, "While there are programs in place to help those with learning disabilities, there are none federally mandated for the gifted" (2014). Therefore, offer your support in getting the instruction the student may need.

If you notice a gifted and talented student on your roster, meet with his parents before the school year begins. Get a chance to know the parents and what they envision for their child. What are the child's strengths; what are his challenges? Find out the child's interests and pursuits.

Meet with gifted and talented student(s) before the school year begins. How do they envision their learning? What do they want to learn? How do they want to learn it? In meeting with these students, either one on one or together, you will glean creative ideas for all student learning.

Ask parents for ideas and suggestions about their children's talents. In what ways can you continue to hone that talent? How can you help the student to build that talent? What can the student do to complete assessments creatively and authentically, other than with traditional paper and pencil? Be creative and open to parent suggestions.

Ask students to explain what they are doing in class to their parents. If they share it with some level of enthusiasm versus indifference, then you have strong evidence the work is at their level. If they use any variation of the word *bored*, dig for more information: Why are they bored? What makes the work boring? What would they rather do? The outcome of this conversation determines your next step.

Encourage students to participate. Students labeled "gifted and talented" often feel uncomfortable participating for fear they may be wrong. They see "challenges, mistakes and even the need to exert effort as threats to their ego rather than as opportunities to improve" (Dweck, 2015). Participating in class is one way to help students become part of a class culture centered on community and collaboration.

CONCLUSION

As you read about the three categories of students, you will notice that, even though they are listed under specific academic labels, the recommendations are interchangeable for *all* students. Always being open to learning is good practice for supporting our gray-area students; in truth, it is also good practice for all students. Likewise, encouraging all students to participate is solid preparation for our gifted and talented students; it also hones the communication skills of all students.

For the sake of our students, let's move beyond the way it's always been to the way it should be. Whether students have labels or not doesn't matter; what does matter is creating opportunities of learning and leading toward lives of growth and grace.

HOW TO USE CHAPTER 1

Book Study Reflection Questions

1. How do you already support special education students, gray-area students, and gifted and talented students?

   - Is there a particular suggestion you already use?
   - If so, how do you use it with your student or students?
   - If not, which one could you implement and how?

2. How do you already support your parents?

   - Is there a particular suggestion that you apply when collaborating with parents?
   - If so, which one is it, and how do you use it?
   - If not, which one could you implement and how?

Professional Learning Community Discussion Questions

1. With department members, choose one of the suggestions for special education, gray-area, or gifted and talented students, and determine why the suggestion has merit. Why would the suggestion be important to *your* classroom? Decide on one suggestion that you want to implement in your classroom with a specific student or an entire class. As you implement the suggestion, keep a reflective journal of the glows and grows regarding implementation and the results.
2. Meet with your department members, and share your reflective journal.

   - What were the successes of implementing the suggestion, and why were they successful?
   - What were the challenges of implementing the suggestion, and why were they a challenge?

Professional Development Discussion Questions

1. As a teacher leader, what is one suggestion that you want your teachers to implement? Upon determining the suggestion, create stations

based on that suggestion. Recruit your exemplary teachers who successfully apply the suggestion with their students to showcase how they implement it in the classroom or when meeting with parents. Design a schedule where teachers rotate from station to station, observing exemplary teachers modeling the chosen suggestion.
2. Create an exit ticket requesting teachers to reflect on how they could implement a particular suggestion in their own classrooms or with parents.

Chapter Two

Scaffolding a Lesson Is Just Good Teaching

Be prepared to break down a lesson and create pieces of learning. When each piece is explained, modeled, practiced, and applied, the parts fit together solidly to form a whole of understanding. Too much lecturing, too thick a packet, or too many directions can cause anxiety and disquiet in students. One small step at a time usually works best.

EXAMPLE 1: ANNOTATION

1. Explain

To begin scaffolding a lesson, explain its purpose. Keep the explanation concrete and clear. For the skill of annotation, begin with defining the three parts of annotation: questions, comments, and vocabulary. Explain why annotation is important: It helps students to interact with text, it supports students in comprehending the text, and it gives students the opportunity to learn more about a topic they might know nothing about.

2. Model

Demonstrate how to annotate a brief piece of text. Put the text where all students can see it clearly. Make sure the text is triple-spaced and in 14-point font for ease of reading and writing. Give students the chance to see the markings clearly.

Distribute the text you will be annotating to each student. Explain to students that they should write down exactly what is being labeled. When they are ready to practice this skill on their own, they will use this example as a model. Frey and Fisher (2013) recommend, "Readers who take the time to really read and investigate a text take notes right on the text. They 'read with a pencil' so that they can make notes about their understandings or quickly find evidence when they need it" (p. 15). Read the first sentence, and underline the key word or brief phrase of interest. In the margin, write a question based on the text. Make sure the question is completely written out. Because this is modeling, show the students exactly how a question should look (see figure 2.1). Or if a comment makes more sense, write a complete sentence in the margin of the text. Again, because this is modeling, show the students exactly how a comment should be written.

Next, circle a vocabulary word that you anticipate most students would not know. Encourage help from the students in determining the meaning of the vocabulary word. If students cannot figure out from context clues the meaning of the word, ask them to write the word "Vocabulary" above it and continue annotating. When they come back to the word, ask them to look it

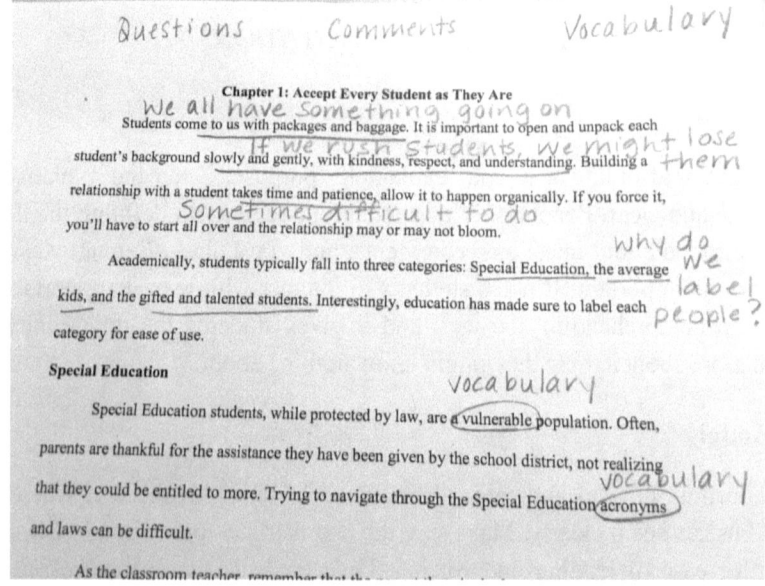

Figure 2.1. Example of Annotation: Questions, Comments, and Vocabulary

up on their mobile devices or a classroom computer or in a dictionary. Write the definition above the vocabulary word.

Continue this practice as a classroom community on the next sentence. Take your time and stop occasionally to survey the students to make sure they are writing down the questions, comments, and vocabulary on their own printouts. Then ask students to help you for the remainder of the article. Ask for volunteers to share their ideas on how to write a question or construct a comment. Write down what the students say. Often, teachers paraphrase student responses, but in this case, write down student responses exactly so they know that their answers are accurately aligned to the text. For students who are unsure of what to ask or how to comment or who initially might need extra support in creating questions and comments, consider distributing the following question and comment starters.

Question Starters for Annotation

1. I wonder why _____.
2. Why is _____ significant?
3. What will happen if he/she _____?
4. Does he/she know/understand _____?

Comment Starters for Annotation

1. This reminds me of the time I _____.
2. I like this situation/person because _____. I don't like this situation/person because _____.
3. I would never do that because _____.
4. I agree with _____ because _____. I disagree with _____ because _____.

3. Practice

When the demonstration is complete, hand out a brief, informational article, perhaps four or five sentences long. Depending on students' reading levels, distribute several versions of the same text. Put students in pairs so they can work together. Fisher, Frey, and Rothenberg (2008) state, "Although guided instruction is teacher led, this does not mean that students are not talking. They use talk to ask questions—of the teacher, of peers, and of themselves—

as well as to clarify understanding, provide feedback to a partner, and reflect once more on their learning" (p. 12).

4. Apply

Walk around the classroom, making sure the students' models are clearly available so they can refer to them when creating their own questions and comments. As students read the first sentence, ask them to create a question or write a comment or circle an unknown word. Give students time to talk with their partners and come to a consensus about what to write. Encourage students to write a complete question or a complete sentence for a comment.

Also, consider color-coding for our visual learners. Before students begin the annotation process, hand out green, red, and blue pens to all students so they can write their questions in green, their comments in red, and vocabulary in blue.

As students create their questions and comments and circle unknown vocabulary words, they will have a visual image of how they are marking their reading and what they have already mastered or where they may need more support. As they practice this technique, they will become stronger readers and, most importantly, stronger thinkers. Depending on their abilities, this universally designed lesson gives all students an opportunity to be a part of the learning. Consider the student who is a linear thinker; they may have difficulty creating conceptually based questions, but they may be able to create "why" comments using the comment starters. Answering the questions may prove difficult, but being part of a collaborative group means the learning is spread equally among all members, who support one another in their comprehension.

EXAMPLE 2: NOTE TAKING

Now that annotation is complete, consider the technique of explain, model, practice, and apply in note taking. Note taking is a highly coveted skill that is a precursor (much like annotation) to finding main ideas and details. All students, regardless of their abilities, can learn to take notes. While the text used to practice note taking may vary depending on the students' abilities, the skill remains the same.

1. Explain

As with any introduction, explain why note taking is important: It helps students to remember information; it assists students in studying for tests; it keeps information organized. Keep your explanation straightforward and uncomplicated.

2. Model

Demonstrate how to create two columns for efficient note taking (see figure 2.2). Platt (2013) explains, "Formal note taking is more about scaffolding the key processes of synthesizing and making meaning from information. It's a tool to remind the reader to stop after every paragraph and think."

Next, distribute blank, lined paper to each student. Together, as a classroom community, draw two columns on the sheet of paper. Make sure the left column is thinner than the right column. Label the left column "Vocabulary" or "Questions" or "Key Words." Then, label the right side "Definitions" or "Answers" or "Notes," respectively (see figure 2.3).

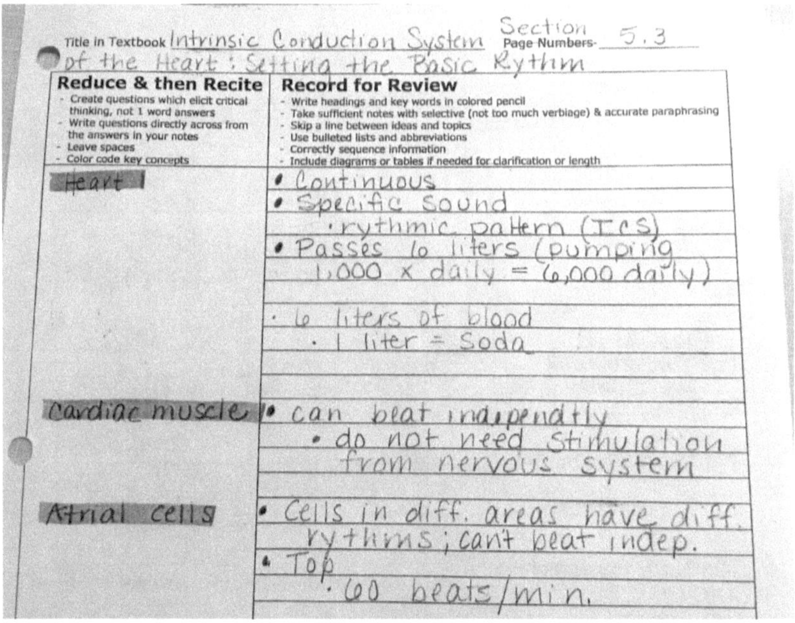

Figure 2.2. **Example of Two-Column Notes to Capture One's Thinking**

Question Starters for Note Taking

1. Who is this _____ about?
2. What is the name of the/this _____ ?
3. Where/When does the _____ take place?
4. Why is the/this _____ important?

3. Practice

Hand out a brief, informational article, perhaps four or five sentences long. Depending on students' reading levels, distribute several versions of the same text. Encourage students to work together based on the same article; in

Topic: Vocabulary	Definitions

Figure 2.3.   Two-Column Notes Form

that way, they can discuss their note taking and share ideas and critiques of their note-taking skills.

4. Apply

As students read their articles, ask them to write down one new word under the "Vocabulary" label. Then ask them to give a sound, educated guess of the word's definition in the "Definitions" column. Give students the opportunity to talk about the word and possible definitions. If students are unable to come to a consensus about a word, ask them to look it up on their mobile devices or a classroom computer or in a dictionary and put the correct definition in the "Definitions" column.

As students continue to read their articles, ask them to write down a question about what they read under the "Questions" column. Offer sentence starters depending on the ability of the students, such as "Who is the article about?" or "When did the situation take place?" or "Why is this information important?" Then, give students time to answer their questions in the "Answers" column. Again, encourage conversation as students create a variety of questions based on sentence starters.

As students finish their articles, ask them to briefly summarize the article under "Questions/Main Ideas" and write down what they perceive as the key word that best summarizes the article under "Key Word." Then ask students to write a complete sentence or two explaining the main idea of the article under "Notes."

This basic technique of explain, model, practice, and apply can be used in all courses and for all student abilities. Try this same procedure in a biology class with sophomores or in an English class focusing on Shakespeare's (2004) *The Tragedy of Romeo and Juliet*. Revise the headings to fit the particular course and the abilities of students (see figure 2.4).

STUDENT IMPLEMENTATION OF THE LESSON

As the classroom teacher, stay focused on the goal of the lesson. What is the learning intention? It might be to explain and model during the first part of the week and practice and apply during the latter half of the week. Allow sufficient time to practice these skills in the classroom. Do not assign annotation or note taking for homework; rather, give students opportunities to show their processing as they work on annotation and note taking in class. In that

Topic/Essential Question:	
	Name: _____
	Class: _____ Period: _____
	Date: _____
Questions/Main Ideas:	Notes:
Summary:	

Figure 2.4. Two-Column Notes Form: Questions and Main Ideas

way, they are able to ask questions, share ideas, and offer suggestions on their own progression.

Furthermore, encourage discussion as students work in pairs or teams. Give students the opportunity to metacognitively share their thinking about thinking. Often it is assumed that, when students are talking, they are off task; in truth, many students talk through what they are doing as a way to process next steps.

During student work time, ask for a volunteer to share her annotations or note taking with the class. Students can see the work of this peer, but most importantly, the student facilitator is able to demonstrate her thinking process and how she created her responses. Students will see that answers may vary and that the "right" answer could be subjective.

TRY A WRITING LESSON

Students appreciate methodical structure. After you have focused on annotation and note taking, consider moving toward a writing lesson. There are many ways to introduce academic paragraph writing. Instead of going through numerous PowerPoint slides explaining how to write a paragraph, give students the opportunity to verbally demonstrate it. Even before students are taught the names of each part of a paragraph or what the parts do, give them the chance to figure it out on their own.

For example, create teams of five students. Give each team an exemplar paragraph, and ask them to label the parts: the topic sentence, the plot reference (the background), the evidence, the analysis, and the transition. Then, give each group time to explain the purpose of the individual parts and why the parts are important. What do they do to create meaning within the paragraph? What happens if one part is missing? Why is their order important in making meaning? This student conversation is more powerful than the teacher explaining each paragraph part in a lecture.

Similarly, cut an exemplar paragraph into pieces: the topic sentence, the plot reference, the evidence, the analysis, and the transition. Then, give the pieces of the essay to each group. Have students line up in the correct sequential order according to the paragraph parts they were given. Students are using a kinesthetic approach to paragraph writing and applying the structure of a paragraph in a social, kinesthetic way. Once again, give the group time to explain the importance of their order. Why did students put themselves in this particular sequential order? What happens when one part (one student) is missing?

Also, when distributing the various parts of the paragraph to the five-member teams, consider using colored paper for each part. The topic sentence could be a strip of red paper; the brief plot reference might be a piece of orange paper; the evidence could be yellow; the analysis might be green; and the transition could be blue. Perhaps use the colors of the rainbow (think the acronym Roy G. Biv—or at least part of the acronym) to help visual learners remember the structure of the paragraph and bring it back from memory when they are writing.

CONCLUSION

Scaffolding lessons for students' abilities is just good teaching. Scaffolding assists students in getting to their goals—whether the goal is learning how to interact with text or to become better note takers. Students' abilities are given priority, and in-class practice, with teacher support, shows students how those skills can be transferred to other situations and other experiences, and in so doing, they are able to stretch their thinking to encompass new learning opportunities.

HOW TO USE CHAPTER 2

Book Study Reflection Questions

1. Do you teach annotation in your classroom? If so, share with your colleagues how you teach it. Now, use the explain, model, practice, and apply method focusing on questions, comments, and vocabulary for annotation. Discuss the successes and challenges of your method and the explain, model, practice, and apply method.
2. Do you teach two-column note taking in your classroom? If so, share with your colleagues how you teach it. Now, use the explain, model, practice, and apply method of two-column note taking. Discuss the successes and challenges of your method and the explain, model, practice, and apply method.

Professional Learning Community Discussion Questions

1. Within departments, choose one of the skills highlighted: annotation or two-column note taking. Implement the chosen skill using the explain, model, practice, and apply method. As you teach the skill to your students, give them an opportunity to share written feedback about the method with you. In addition, keep a reflective journal highlighting the successes and challenges of teaching this skill using the explain, model, practice, and apply method. Meet with your department, and share your students' written feedback and your reflective journal.

- What were the students' successes of implementing the skill using the prescribed method, and why were they successful?
- What were the students' challenges of implementing the suggestion, and why were they a challenge?
- What were your successes of implementing the skill using the prescribed method, and why were they successful?
- What were your challenges of implementing the skill using the prescribed method, and why were they a challenge?

2. Determine, as a department, a specific method you will implement for building skills. As a result, students will benefit from the continuity of learning a particular skill.

Professional Development Discussion Questions

1. As the teacher leader, what is one skill that you want your teachers to implement? Upon determining the skill, ask each department to create a lesson for the skill within their content areas, employing the explain, model, practice, and apply method. Record each department demonstrating the skill within their content areas. Showcase two or three departments employing the explain, model, practice, and apply method.
2. Begin building a "Best Practices" library where teachers can view videos of their colleagues teaching research-based skills.

Chapter Three

Responding to Every Student

Every day, all students will have a problem—or something they perceive to be a problem. Stop, look, and listen. Don't offer a solution until invited to do so. Don't minimize their problems, experiences, or situations. Don't take their problems to the principal or another administrator until you've given the student time to think it through. Sometimes all they want is to be heard.

Whether a student's problem is perceived or real doesn't matter. That problem can become all-consuming to that student. The most engaging and meaningful lesson can become background noise if the student is unable to concentrate. Therefore, you must be ready to stop and create a situation where you are uniquely focused on that student. You must be willing to put aside whatever it is you are working on to look at the student and connect. Finally, you must be prepared to listen, avoiding judgment or forming an opinion. The goal is to get the student back to learning as quickly as possible without escalating an already-unpredictable situation.

STOP, LOOK, AND LISTEN

Stop

A student may purposely seek you out if he is experiencing a difficult situation. Or you may notice a student's negative behavior when entering your classroom. Either way, you have the opportunity to comfort the student, help him develop a new mind-set, and hopefully begin his day again.

First, stop what you are doing. Don't continue taking attendance or finish grading a paper or revising a lesson plan. Stop and acknowledge the student's feelings. You know when your students are distressed: "colorful" verbal language, tense body language, or subtle tears are just a few signs that students are distraught.

Next, when you notice these behaviors, offer a greeting using the student's name. According to Rita Kohli, "Names have incredible significance to families, with so much thought, meaning and culture woven into them" (quoted in McLaughlin, 2016). Using a student's name "can be a powerful link to their identity" (2016); therefore, pronouncing it accurately is a sign of respect and reverence. This seemingly small gesture lets the student know you are connecting directly with him.

What It Looks Like

Mike was a tough kid: rough around the edges and totally disengaged from school. You could tell, when he stomped into the classroom 10 minutes late, something was wrong. He was angry; his face was contorted and red. He stormed to his desk and sat down with a thump. Ms. Timm looked at him, said "Good morning, Mike," smiled, and continued explaining the morning's goal, along with the pertinent skills. She asked students to take out paper along with their texts.

Mike did nothing. Ms. Timm gave him a couple of sheets of paper and a pencil. He moved them aside and put his head down. Ms. Timm stood next to him and gently gave the next set of directions. As students were moving their desks to make teams, Ms. Timm leaned over and encouraged him to move to a group.

Look

Eye contact offers an opportunity to make a connection. Recognizing the student is distressed shows that you are aware of his feelings and will not ignore him. Barati (2015) explains that "longer eye contact is associated with trust, good feelings, and rapport all of which are important" (p. 224). Eye contact confirms your relationship with your students—especially the ones who are particularly despondent.

If the student continues to feel disheartened, ask him to quietly go into the hallway for a private conversation. This gives you a chance to connect with him without other students' looking and wondering. You need to give the student a chance to share his concern, if he wants to, in a nonthreatening atmosphere.

What It Looks Like

"Leave me alone!" he shouted into the crook of his arm. A few heads turned in their direction.

"Mike," Ms. Timm said softly, "join Devon's group. You can follow along with him." He lifted up his head. "I told you, leave me alone! Shut up and leave me alone!" he screamed.

Before the situation escalated further or the language turned colorful, Ms. Timm said, "Mike, let's go into the hallway for a minute." The teacher turned to her class and asked them to please review their vocabulary notecards.

Mike stood up with such force that his desk tipped over. Ms. Timm followed him into the hallway, where he paced back and forth. Ms. Timm gently closed the classroom door about halfway—wide enough to see and hear her class but narrow enough to give Mike the attention he deserved.

Listen

As you stand in the hallway with your student, don't ask what's wrong. That answer will come in time. You really don't need to know what happened—at least not yet. The situation will reveal itself eventually. At this moment, your goal is to respect your student's authentic feelings.

When the student begins to share his concerns, don't correct his language, and don't correct his feelings. Focus solely on him, and listen. Because you want this conversation to stay between you and the student, keep the conversation discreet and respectful.

What It Looks Like

"OK, what do you need from me?" Right then, Ms. Timm needed to know how she could get her student to a place of learning. Mike stopped, looked at his teacher, and began ranting about his mother. There had been a disagreement that morning, and he left the house angry, hurt, and frustrated.

Ms. Timm listened and kept quiet. She kindly reminded Mike to keep his voice down because she didn't want to bother the students working in the classroom or alert administration. The teacher didn't want Mike to feel that his honesty would get him in trouble. This didn't need to be another referral. He was angry at his mother, and Ms. Timm was the first adult female he saw that morning. When she asked him to join a group, Ms. Timm was one more person asking one more thing of an already-stressed and disenfranchised kid.

As you listen, it is common to formulate mental questions or think of how you might want to express your responses or interrupt to share your insights and ideas. But when you think of questions, responses, or insights, you miss what the student is saying. Avoid interrupting so the student can complete his thought and you can stay attentive to the whole conversation.

According to Wagner (2017), "Our minds can wander a bit when we're listening to someone. It doesn't mean what's being said isn't important, but it does mean that when you sense this happening it's time to re-focus your attention back onto the speaker." Refocusing or recommitting our attention back to the speaker shows students that we are completely present in their feelings and trying to understand their distress.

Summing It Up

Stop, look, and listen are done almost simultaneously. But if you think of them as three distinct steps, you will be more apt to recognize the necessity of including all three. If you don't stop or look but only listen with an occasional "uh huh," that student may feel neglected and dismissed. As a result, he may forego coming to you next time or, worse, decide not to share his concerns at all.

It's vital that students have an adult with whom they feel respected, welcomed, and connected. Supporting students through "Stop, Look, and Listen" gives them what they need to be engaged learners with problems and concerns that hopefully can be managed.

SEEKING SOLUTIONS, PERCEIVING PROBLEMS, AND ALERTING ADMINISTRATION—OR NOT

Every day your students need you—emotionally, behaviorally, and mentally. As an educator, you look for ways to support them and often have to make quick decisions based on your conversations with them. Depending on the student, you might want to offer some helpful suggestions to alleviate his trepidation—or not. The following are some things to consider as you talk with your student—with two different approaches for each action.

Don't Offer a Solution

Don't offer a solution. It would be easy to say, "Well, if I were you, I would do this" or "Next time, you need to . . ." because, that's what we want to do—we want to fix the issue at hand. However, some problems cannot be fixed by you. They must be thought through and wrestled with before a solution is possible. Give the student the chance to grapple with his problem.

Don't offer classic clichés. Phrases like "Things will be better tomorrow" or "Look on the bright side" are just words. They mean nothing to the troubled student, and they only show that we are not taking his feelings seriously.

Finally, be aware of pithy comments like "You will be exactly as happy as you decide to be" or "To plant a garden is to believe in tomorrow." While you may think you are offering profound wisdom, your student will be frustrated by the lack of connection to *his* concerns. Be careful that your comments do not sound condescending. These are real feelings your student is experiencing; therefore, allow the student to think through possible outcomes.

Don't "should" the student into something you think he must do. When you use *should*, you impose your sense of right or wrong on the student. When you advise the student with "You should do this," you take away the student's power to create a reasonable solution. Instead, give the student a chance to create a successful outcome based on his ability to reflect and ruminate.

Offer a Solution

As the student is sharing the situation or experience, perhaps a solution is obvious and the student simply doesn't see it. As you and the student are standing in the hallway in conversation, grab a chair, clipboard, and pen. Give the student a chance to share her frustrations.

At the top of the paper, ask the student to write down the problem; a variety of examples are available in figure 3.1. Then draw a T-chart with the phrase "My Feelings" on the left side and "Why I Feel This Way" on the right side. Give the student time to write out her emotions and why she feels the way she does. This is a way for the student to label her feelings and acknowledge them. This powerful exercise helps the student to realize the importance of her feelings and to discern why she feels the way she does.

Don't Minimize the Problem

The student's problem is significant. It is so important, in fact, that it has disrupted the student from learning in your classroom. As a result, her problem deserves to have meaningful discussion. Be aware of your body language as you are listening. Don't eye-roll, sigh, fidget, or look at the clock.

I am angry because: _____

My Feelings	Why I Feel This Way

My best friend hurt my feelings because: _____

My Feelings	Why I Feel This Way

I am hurt because: _____

My Feelings	Why I Feel This Way

My weekend was hard because: _____

My Feelings	Why I Feel This Way

Figure 3.1. Reflective Thinking Form

You are giving this student your undivided attention so she can solve the problem.

Minimizing it or treating it as anything but important says to the student that her problems aren't significant. One can argue that a person's problem is a matter of perception, and that's true. However, this matter is affecting that student right now. It is paralyzing the student, preventing her from being an active member of a learning community. Therefore, the perception is real and must be treated as a real problem in need of a real solution.

Decrease the Problem

As you and the student are talking about the problem, share with the student how important his learning is to you. In addition, explain that the lesson you prepared was designed with this student in mind. As a result, you want him in your classroom, learning as soon as possible.

Ask the student what you can do to get him back in class. Can discussion about the problem be tabled for now but revisited at lunch or during study hall or after school? If so, ask the student to come back and talk with you. If the student is able to go back into class and be an active participant, then the problem may have lost some of its steam. But if the student does come back later in the day, listen and decide your next move. Will the discussion help solve the problem, or should you seek out support?

Don't Seek an Administrator

You can certainly send the student to the office—but he will miss more learning. If your school has a safety officer, you can ask him to remove the student, but to what end? If you were to do any of those things, it would be difficult for the student to trust you again and difficult to believe that classroom community is a goal.

Don't seek an administrator. Don't write a referral. Tell the student that the goal of this conversation is to ultimately get him back to your class for learning. Therefore, what can be done right now to put this situation away so the student can return to the classroom? Ask the student if he would write down his frustrations. Would a walk to the water fountain help?

The student may be unable to tell you what he needs. At that point, a quiet space may help. If possible, ask a colleague to stay with your class. Take the student to a nearby quiet space and sit with the student, helping him to practice some deep-breathing exercises. This quiet time may naturally help the student's state of mind.

Seek an Administrator

In some situations, you need the support of an administrator, school safety officer, school psychologist, or school social worker. Do not hesitate to ask for support from these individuals. They have been trained for difficult situations where specific legal documents may be necessary.

Tell the student that you need to bring in an administrator to this conversation and explain why. You must be transparent as you clarify your reasons. While the student may become even more heated or frustrated, it is time to seek assistance to keep the situation controlled and the student safe.

CONCLUSION

Imagine the courage it takes for students to share their pain with us. Because you are an authentic and respectful listener, the student feels safe to be honest and genuine with you. Use these suggestions as opportunities to create students of character, compassion, and contentment.

HOW TO USE CHAPTER 3

Book Study Reflection Questions

1. Do you explicitly stop, look, and listen with your students when they are feeling overwhelmed? If so, share with your colleagues how you apply the method. If you do not, what method works for your students?
2. What are the positives and negatives of the stop, look, and listen method? Share with your colleagues.
3. Share some situations where you have offered a solution and where you have not offered a solution. Explain why you choose one over the other and the consequences of your decision.
4. Share some situations where you did not minimize a problem and where you did decrease a problem. Explain why you choose one over the other and the consequences of your decision.

5. Share some situations where you did not seek an administrator and where you did seek an administrator. Explain why you choose one over the other and the consequences of your decision.

Professional Learning Community Discussion Questions

1. Within departments, explain what you do to help students feel validated when they are feeling distressed.
2. Give examples of how teachers can apply the stop, look, and listen method. Ask teachers to demonstrate stop, look, and listen for their colleagues.
3. Within your department, place teachers into three groups. The first group is "offer a solution/do not offer a solution," the second group is "do not minimize a problem/decrease a problem," and the third group is "do not seek an administrator/seek an administrator." Ask each group to create a scenario or use an authentic scenario and apply their topic to that scenario.

    - What are the successes, challenges, and possible consequences of how the group chooses to address a problem?
    - What can your department do to ensure that distressed students feel validated?

4. Share your conversation and learning with other departments.

Professional Development Discussion Questions

1. As the teacher leader, reflect on how you apply the stop, look, and listen method with your faculty and staff. When and how do you explicitly apply stop, look, and listen to your faculty and staff? Share your reflection with faculty and staff.
2. Create groups of five. Do not create groups based on departments; rather, encourage faculty and staff to collaborate with colleagues not in their departments. Give each group a challenging scenario based on situations you have been involved in. Ask each group to apply either "did not seek an administrator" or "seek an administrator" to the particular scenario. Share the scenario and the groups' decisions with other groups. Ask groups to provide feedback.

- Why did your group choose that particular response?
- Would you change your response based on the feedback?

Chapter Four

Students Want to Feel Loved

Your students want to feel like they're the only ones in your class, on your caseload, or in your heart. A small token of appreciation—a handwritten note, a quiet teacher–student lunch, or handing out your cell phone number—shows students you care about them and their academics. The importance of building relationships cannot be overstressed; students need you to show them that love is always possible.

PERIMETER PEOPLE

It's not unusual to have a student in class who doesn't seem to fit in, who might seem uncomfortable or have idiosyncratic behaviors. One of the greatest challenges facing education today are "disengaged students [who] rarely see any relevance or usefulness in whatever is being taught" (Cutler, 2016). What can we do to gather those students, embrace them, and support their emotions and learning?

Imagine this scenario: You have created what you believe to be the best lesson in the world. The learning intention is written in specific, student-friendly language. The success criteria are achievable and measurable. The skills are based on standards, and the strategies are engaging and motivating. After the lesson, 98 percent of the class told you through their reflective exit ticket that they could explain to you what they learned that day and that they enjoyed the lesson. Ah, success!

But what about the 2 percent of students who didn't respond favorably? Are those the students who are feeling disaffected? The students who, while it's not necessarily a bad thing, don't want to be the center of attention? Are those statistics satisfactory enough for you to deem the lesson a success? The following tips can move students from the perimeter to the heart of the classroom.

Be Human

When a student is disengaged, don't call her out in front of her peers; wait until class is over and keep the conversation light and friendly, not defensive. Don't ask her why she wasn't participating. Let her know you want her to think about joining in. Maybe you won't see participation right away, but she might eventually begin to seek you out before school or after school to share and exchange ideas. If so, use that time to discover her interests and concerns.

Julia's Story: The Problem

During my third year of teaching freshman English at an all-girls private high school, I met Julia. She had been home-schooled all of her academic career. Julia was quiet to a debilitating degree, yet her assignments and assessments demonstrated her understanding of the material. When called on, she was mute. In small groups, she would offer a grin but added nothing. It was becoming more and more obvious that something was amiss.

One day, I saw her sitting next to her locker during lunch. After gentle conversation and respectful nudging, I learned that Julia had no one to eat lunch with and she had been eating alone in the basement for most of the school year.

Do Whatever It Takes

During conversation, try to find something that suggests an interest in the student. Does she have any siblings? Does she have any pets? Reviewing the completed family survey (see textbox 6.2) might help to find some commonalities between you and the student. Keep the conversation light and casual. The intent is to get to know each other and to determine how to bring the student away from the perimeter and toward the heart of the learning.

Julia's Story: The Meeting

I asked Julia to have lunch with me the next day so we could get to know each other. She gratefully accepted. I began with light conversation, asking what movies she liked and if she had any brothers or sisters. Did she have any pets? After every question, I answered, too. "I like comedies; I have two brothers and one cat." She answered my questions but didn't elaborate. I asked her to join me the next day.

Break Bread Together

When you eat lunch with a student, remember to stay centered on the value of the interaction: the importance of sharing one's thinking. Then, let them practice how to participate in class. Ask questions you will ask the next day. Give the student a chance to prepare her responses prior to class tomorrow, all while enjoying a wonderful lunch with you.

Julia's Story: The Practice

As Julia and I were eating our lunches and homemade chocolate chip cookies, I explained to her that I would be introducing Poe's (2006) "The Cask of Amontillado" tomorrow. I handed the story to her and read the first two lines.

I asked her what she thought the lines meant, and she responded that the main character must be angry. She spent the next 10 minutes explaining aloud what she was thinking. I encouraged her to track her thinking by taking bulleted notes on some of her ideas.

I told Julia I would ask the same questions tomorrow and also asked if she would share her bulleted notes with the class. She could securely share her insights and ideas. She nodded, but I wasn't sure if she would really participate in class.

Make a Deal

Ask the student to offer just one comment or idea during the class period. Keep track of her remarks with a check mark, and show her that you are keeping track so she knows the value of her contribution. Don't expect her to suddenly become a chatterbox. As the weeks progress, request more comments per class, upping the ante. Remember, she has to get something out of the deal, too. Don't forget to call home to share the positive participation news with family members.

Julia's Story: The Execution

The next day in class, I distributed the story. I saw Julia shifting uncomfortably in her chair. After reading the first few lines out loud, I asked students if they had any insight to share. I saw Julia reach for her notes.

Several hands went up. Julia looked at me and then timidly raised her hand. Using her notes, Julia responded, hesitatingly at first, but when I encouraged students to jot down what she was saying, her confidence grew. As I walked around the room, listening to student analysis, I saw a student tap Julia on the arm and lean over to mutter something to her. Julia beamed.

Acceptance Is Not Resignation

Some students might not participate or engage in the way that you want them to. At that point, you have to accept their boundaries. Your idea of participation and engagement and a student's idea of participation and engagement are (probably) different. However, you have made your expectations clear that participation is important, and you have given a student the opportunity to share her ideas—even if it wasn't with a class of her peers.

Julia's Story: The Closure

Julia and I had sporadic lunch dates for the next couple of weeks. As her confidence grew in class, so did her ability to participate and share her thoughts in small groups. Julia's eagerness and willingness to participate in class helped to create an even more favorable classroom community.

By the end of first quarter, Julia had found her niche—three other homeschooled girls were also in our school and had the same lunch period. Julia never ate lunch alone again.

SMALL CHOICES; BIG LOVE

Giving students choices is another way to show the love. Offering choices doesn't have to be complicated. Choice can be as simple as giving students opportunities to pick the day for an upcoming checkup, or assessment (see chapter 7). For example, tell students that you would like to assess them on some of the work they have been doing in class. You pick the week, but let them pick the day of that week. When they pick the day, make sure you are clear in telling them that, because they are picking the day, they own the responsibility of being successful. What day did they want to demonstrate their understanding? Give students power in choosing the checkup day because they know their personal and academic calendars better than you do.

If the majority of students have an extracurricular activity scheduled on a Tuesday, then perhaps schedule the checkup on Thursday. Or, if the majority of students know ahead of time that they are scheduled to have an English test on Thursday, then schedule your checkup for Tuesday. Let them choose the day that works best for *them*. This control gives them confidence in their learning and empowerment in their knowledge. In making this choice, your students assume responsibility for their learning. You are merely the facilitator guiding them toward a successful outcome of their decision. The following are some ways to offer choice in the secondary classroom.

Science Example: Introducing the Virus Unit

Locate three articles with different reading levels introducing viruses. Give students the chance to choose the article they want to read instead of assigning a whole class one article. As Allington and Gabriel (2012) explain, "Students read more, understand more, and are more likely to continue reading when they have the opportunity to choose what they read."

English/ELA Example: Analyzing *The Catcher in the Rye*

As students are reading the story of Holden Caulfield, give them the opportunity to choose how they will demonstrate the themes of the novel (Salinger, 1951). They could write an analysis paper about the themes, give a speech highlighting the themes, debate the complexity of one theme versus another, or present another student-devised project.

Humanities Example: Define the Consequences of the Cold War

Upon completing a chapter on the Cold War, ask students to show their understanding of the consequences of the Cold War. They could use a graphic organizer to map the effects and their consequences, present a time line showing the progression of the Cold War, dress up as John F. Kennedy and Nikita Khrushchev and debate the effects of the Cold War, or present another student-devised project.

Math Example: Introducing Numbers and Operations

As students are practicing numbers and operations, ask them to apply what they have learned so far. They could create a human number system, asking the class to participate; draw a diagram that illustrates the relationships among the different sets of numbers; apply manipulative materials that help make multiplication and division with integers more tangible; or present another student-devised project.

Physical Education Example: Ultimate Frisbee Assessment

Give students a choice of assessments, such as physically demonstrating how to play ultimate frisbee, drawing a comic strip illustrating how to play ultimate frisbee, writing a rap highlighting the moves associated with ultimate frisbee, or presenting another student-devised project.

Music Example: Musical Vocabulary Practice

After students have defined basic music vocabulary, give them opportunities to practice the definitions. They could create a song with the words and definitions and teach it to the class; organize a flash mob, where one student says the word and the other students in the mob respond with the definition; produce a music video highlighting the words and their definitions; or present another student-devised project.

World Language Example: Using Common Words in Sentences

As students are practicing common household words, give them a chance to use those words in real-world situations. They could create signs with a word and tape the word to the corresponding object around the school, teach a "word of the day" to students over the PA system every morning, record themselves in their neighborhoods saying the name of an object, or present another student-devised project.

Art Example: Artist Study

Students must research an artist of their choice and present their artists to the class. They could dress up like the artist and present a biography, create an original piece of art based on the artist's techniques and share the techniques with the class, write an original piece of music sharing the life of the artist, or present another student-devised project.

CONCLUSION

Loving every student can seem overwhelming, but within that love is the opportunity to give your students what they might be lacking. Even a simple "Good morning" and a smile can demonstrate your willingness to be there for them and to offer a respite of caring.

Within the language of love is the prospect for choice. Allowing choice shows that you trust your students enough that they will make the choice that suits them best. While they may need a gentle nudge or a slight persuasion, the choices you offer are always in their best interests and meant solely for them and their learning—the ultimate gift of love and understanding.

HOW TO USE CHAPTER 4

Book Study Reflection Questions

1. How do you encourage participation and engagement in all of your students?
2. What happens when students don't participate?
3. Do you have a "Julia" in your class? If so, how did you connect with her or him?
4. What does choice look like in your class? Give an example of how you offer choice to your students.

Professional Learning Community Discussion Questions

1. With department members, share how you encourage participation and engagement in your students.
2. With department members, share examples of interventions you use when students don't participate.
3. On a piece of poster paper, give examples of how your department members offer choice in their classrooms. Share your examples with other departments. What do you notice? What are successes and challenges? Ask departments to use a choice example from another depart-

ment and report on its successes or challenges at the next professional learning community meeting.

Professional Development Discussion Questions

1. As the teacher leader, how do you encourage participation, engagement, and leadership in your staff?
2. As the teacher leader, what are some ways you encourage the "Julias" on your staff?
3. How do you encourage your colleagues to create classrooms of choice?
4. Give examples of how you offer choice to your colleagues.
5. Share the article "The Top Five Reasons We Love Giving Students Choice in Reading" (Skeeters et al., 2016) with your staff. Ask them to share two or three ideas that they could implement in their classroom.

Chapter Five

Empathy, Equality, and Equity

There will always be another way to teach a lesson or a different way to write a checkup (a checkup is an assessment—see chapter 7). But, what always remains is your genuine love and concern for your students. Any less than your absolute presence in the classroom shortchanges them and the valuable work you do on their behalf. Therefore, trying to understand every student's negative behavior or offering differentiated choices to *all* students illustrates empathy, equality, and equity.

EMPATHY

Building relationships with students is one of the most important things you will do. While content and skill building are certainly crucial to learning, students will not learn—and, more importantly, will not care to learn—if they feel you do not care about them. Showing empathy does not mean giving in to every student whim or demand. Showing empathy means that you will model compromise and compassion. It means being human.

It's easy to assign homework and give checkups, but you want to go beyond that; you want to build a classroom community. Within that community are your students, but to be the teacher you want to be, they are no longer *just* your students; they are your academic family. As a result, you are protective, impassioned, and decidedly human.

Often, students who are academically behind are those who will act out most. Their acting out is not based on being evil human beings. DeCostella, Byrne, and Covington (2013) explain that some students "lack confidence but rather than seeking to prevent failure, they aim instead to reduce its 'implications.' They do so by adopting strategies that deflect the causes of failure away from their ability" (p. 12). Simply put, it is important for these students to save themselves from embarrassment by any means possible; therefore, if acting out means that they won't have to humiliate themselves by reading text that is too difficult or solving a problem that is too tough, so be it.

When teachers ask you about the behavior of one of your students, it's usually because the student is acting out in their particular classes. Don't fall into the trap of responding, and don't run to the office to read the student's cumulative folder. Rather, make your own assessment based on the student's personality and the relationship you have with her. You want to get to know the student on her own terms, not based on a report written by someone you don't know about someone whom you just met and founded on a situation that happened in the past. Upon meeting your students on that first day of school, tell them everyone (including you) will begin with a clean slate. In that way, you and your students will learn together, grow together, and—at times—fail together. Remember, a family protects each other. That is how it survives, grows, and shows empathy to each member and to itself.

EQUALITY

Your students want to be treated fairly in your classroom. They want you to be just and impartial. If they perceive favoritism or preference, they will never trust you. It is that simple.

Your students want to do well. While some might have had negative encounters with education, most will try again. Because of their sheer will to physically attend and mentally contemplate, you owe them the most engaging and motivating lessons you can write. However, remember that too much information causes anxiety and concern. Giving students the tools to dig into something they are interested in or something they have a passion for encourages them to research those topics and be self-sufficient learners.

Ask your students what they need. Give everyone an opportunity to share with you what they want to study. Students want to be connected to their learning and in control of it. When planning a lesson, think about the connections students will be able to make. What is relevant to their lives? How can you make your lessons connect with them and their backgrounds? What do they want to read about? What do they want to know right now?

For example, students are often tasked with writing a creative reflection about their last family vacation in English class; however, many students have never gone on a family vacation. The assignment holds no connection to these students and creates a gap between those who have taken a vacation and those who don't have the means or opportunity. As a result, this assignment becomes busywork for some students and another example of cultural inequity. Instead, give students in-class time to write a "Dear Teacher" letter to tell you about their family, their academic backgrounds, or their hobbies (see textbox 5.1). This lesson can work in any class, not just English, and you may be able to apply the letter to your lessons, keeping your students connected to their learning in a very personal way.

Dear Teacher

Gives students an opportunity to share who they are, along with their family, backgrounds, hobbies, and interests.

Dear Teacher,

I want to tell you a little bit about myself.
My family _____.
My extended family (grandparents, godparents, cousins) _____.
My neighborhood _____.

Next, I want to tell you about my hobbies and interests.
I like to go _____.
I like to play _____.
I have fun when I _____.

Finally, I want to tell you about our family traditions.
My family celebrates _____.
My family goes to _____ every year because _____.
My family likes to _____.

Here are some other things about me you might not know: _____.

Sincerely,

Like any family, you asked questions; you listened and created opportunities for success. That is how a family treats everyone equally while being cognizant of differences.

Equity

As stated earlier, students often argue over what's fair and what's right. The real argument is equality versus equity. Many students believe all students deserve the same treatment, same homework, and same assessment, no matter what. To deviate beyond the same shows that you play favorites. However, most teachers and parents understand the difference between equality and equity. According to Safir (2016), "If equality means giving everyone the same resources, equity means giving each student access to the resources they need to learn and thrive." How can you offer equity in your lessons that are fair and right? The following literacy ideas can be revised and modified for all content areas and abilities.

Prereading

Let's say your lesson is about the Birmingham Children's Crusade of 1963. If you were to ask your students what they know about this particular event, many would probably say nothing. But your students probably do know something about the civil rights movement, which is a part of the Birmingham Children's Crusade. They just don't know they know!

Give each student a copy of the "What Do I Already Know?" form (see figure 5.1). Model the prereading strategy for them by asking them to write down "Martin Luther King Jr." in the corresponding alphabetical box. "Martin Luther King Jr." could go in the "M" box or the "K" box.

Ask students to share what they know out loud so their peers can write down their answers, too. Encourage them to write down a key word or a brief phrase. Urge them to try to fill up every box with at least one key word or brief phrase that relates to the topic, in this case the civil rights movement. Then, once all the boxes are complete, ask students to choose one "Thinking Aloud Stem" and write down what they think they will be reading about, writing about, or thinking about, thereby extending the conversation and their learning.

This prereading strategy showcases universal design because all student abilities have been considered; students share how much they know or how little they know without being judged or graded. Perhaps a student has only

AB	CD	EF
GH	IJ	KL
MN	OP	QR
ST	UV	WXYZ

Thinking Aloud Stems:

1. I think . . .

2. Maybe this means . . .

3. I'm guessing . . .

4. This allows me to assume . . .

5. I predict _____ because . . .

Figure 5.1. What Do I Already Know?

heard of Rosa Parks, while another student has a great deal of background on the topic. Either way, all students are able to participate and extend each other's knowledge based on what they know.

This prereading resource can be used as a formative assessment after a lesson. For example, after a reading, ask students to complete the boxes by sharing what they remember. While the task is rudimentary, it would assist students in recalling prior knowledge. In addition, as you are walking around the room, gather specific observational information on students by jotting down notes on who is sharing and who is writing. You may notice that a student has remained quiet or has not added any new information on her grid. This could be an indication of a lack of background knowledge or that the student is unsure how to articulate what she knows. These notes can help to determine the students who may need extra thinking time or extra writing time on future assignments or assessments.

During Reading

Prior to the reading, cut and paste the front page of Gilmore's (2014) article "The Birmingham Children's Crusade of 1963" into a Word document. Then, when students have completed the "What Do I Already Know?" grid, distribute the front page. Briefly demonstrate the skill of annotating the first sentence or two. Encourage students to work in pairs as they annotate for questions, comments, and vocabulary (see chapter 2). Also, for those students who may need help creating questions and comments, distribute the "Annotation Sentence Starters" (see figure 5.2).

After students have completed their annotations, give them the opportunity to share their work with their peers. The "Give Two, Get Two" exercise promotes conversation and collaboration. Ask students to stand up and circulate around the room, providing their classmates with two annotations, while they take two. Those students who need extra confidence in their annotating can look at the work of peers and talk about the questions and comments their peers created. "Give Two, Get Two" highlights an important 21st-century skill of collaboration by encouraging students to drive the conversations. In addition, students will "clarify their understanding, refine their thinking, and synthesize information" (Barnett et al., 2017).

After students have had a chance to share their annotations, the next step is to define any vocabulary they might have marked. Give students time to work with peers to look up vocabulary and make notes in the margins. Once students have annotated the text, what do you want them to do with it? Did they wonder about Janice Kelsey and where she is today? Did students ask questions about what happened at the 16th Street Baptist Church? Do students just want to learn more about the march? Give students research time to learn more about the topics they found interesting. Allow them to share their research with the class in interesting and creative ways. Perhaps students can

Questions	Comments
Why did...?	I notice...
Why is this significant?	I predict...
I wonder why...?	This reminds me of...
What happened when.../if...?	I think...
How does...?	I'm surprised that...
What might happen if...?	I'd like to know...
Do you agree/disagree with...?	I realized...
Why do you think...?	If I were...
Imagine what would happen if...?	I didn't know that...

Figure 5.2. Annotation Sentence Starters

share their information in an imaginative video or an intriguing rap or an inspirational spoken word.

After Reading

Students need the opportunity to reflect on the lesson and how it was structured. Create formative assessments that evaluate the lesson and its *delivery* (see textbox 5.2). Was the lesson delivered in a relevant and meaningful way? If so, it is far more likely to stick. Student feedback is crucial in the creation of vigorous lessons that assess 21st-century skills; therefore, asking students to assess the lesson is giving them the opportunity to apply what they know to what they have learned.

Exit Ticket

Is specific to the lesson being taught and encourages the student to offer feedback on teacher methodology and instruction.

Name: _____
Learning Intention: _____
Success Criteria: _____

Please list three specific concepts you learned today from *What Do I Already Know?* or the *Annotation* lesson:

1. _____

2. _____

3. _____

Give one example of how you can apply a concept that you learned, either academically, personally, or behaviorally: _____

Glows and Grows
Glows: List the instructional methods that you thought **went well** today.

Grows: List ways in which I can **improve** the instructional methods in class.

When administering a reflection, make sure you give the students enough time to complete it. Asking students to specifically offer concepts urges them to metacognitively think about their thinking. What did they specifically learn that could be transferred to other courses or other situations? Meet with students who gave you unfavorable feedback. Your goal is not to intimidate or badger the student into changing his mind; rather, it is a way for you to determine what the student needed and how you can improve your practice.

In addition, encouraging students to offer their glows and grows of the lesson shows them that you value their opinions. However, when giving directions, make sure you explain the purpose of the glows and grows. You want them to think through the lesson, look at their notes, and jot down the successes and challenges. The purpose of the glow is to reinforce the positive work you are already doing. As an example, what are three things that you do well? Perhaps you give students sufficient wait time when asking questions.

Possibly students appreciate your explanations when the material is difficult. Maybe students mentioned that they valued the help you gave them during their research. Whatever their comments regarding your successes, thank them for their positive feedback. The purpose of the grow is to hone your practice; what can you do to move your practice forward? Perhaps students might appreciate more wait time when responding to questions. Possibly students felt your explanations were convoluted. Maybe the research topics they chose proved to be difficult, and your support was unhelpful. Their comments offer powerful results for practical future planning. Review their comments and adjust your practice accordingly.

CONCLUSION

The academic, behavioral, and personal lessons you teach your students cannot be overstressed or overtaught. They are looking to you for the "right" answer, to help them travel the "right" road, and to model the "right" viewpoints. Offering examples of empathy, equality, and equity assists your students in navigating an increasingly perplexing world.

Creating an empathetic, equal, and equitable classroom could be considered a daunting challenge. However, consider the various strategies in this chapter ("Dear Teacher" letter; "What Do I Already Know?"; "Give Two, Get Two"; "Exit Ticket") as a way to implement empathy, equality, and equity without disrupting the classroom objectives. More importantly, consider your authentic classroom as the "right" thing to do for you, your students, and their navigation.

HOW TO USE CHAPTER 4

Book Study Reflection Questions

1. How do you demonstrate empathy in your classroom?
2. How do you demonstrate equality in your classroom?
3. How do you demonstrate equity in your classroom?
4. What are some questions you could add to the exit ticket?
5. How would you follow up an exit ticket that offered suggestions?

Professional Learning Community Discussion Questions

1. Share examples of how your department members demonstrate empathy.
2. Share examples of how your department members demonstrate equality.
3. Share examples of how your department members demonstrate equity.
4. Review the prereading, during reading, and after reading equitable lesson. Offer your ideas on the lesson; what would it look like in your classroom?
5. Consider giving the exit ticket to students, and share the results with fellow department members. What are the results telling you, and how could you implement any student suggestions?

Professional Development Discussion Questions

1. As the teacher leader, how do you demonstrate empathy among your colleagues?
2. As the teacher leader, how do you demonstrate equality among your colleagues?
3. As the teacher leader, how do you demonstrate equity among your colleagues?
4. Encourage teachers to stretch their thinking. Plan a professional development for teachers to practice writing equitable lesson plans to share with their colleagues.
5. Do you offer exit tickets to your colleagues after a professional development? If so, how do you gather results and implement suggestions? If not, ask your colleagues for ideas on what to include in an exit ticket.

Chapter Six

The Community of Family

When talking with family members, offer specific positives and exact concerns about their children's abilities. Be careful of generalizations like *always*, *never*, *usually*, and *sometimes*. Give explicit examples, and partner with parents to create opportunities for growth.

For example, instead of saying something like "It seems that Ani always has to go to the bathroom when we begin our math lesson," maybe say, "I notice that when we begin our math lesson, Ani wants to go to the restroom. I'm wondering if she is anxious about math. What do you think?" In truth, we need to find out why Ani is getting up to leave class at that time; perhaps it's more of an avoidance of math than having to really use the restroom. But by phrasing the comment in this way, you invite family members to help you determine the problem and to offer their help and expertise. Family members want to support teachers—show them how.

Family members are familiar with traditional communication styles, such as the iconic parent–teacher conference meant to share their children's progress. However, the parent–teacher conference is an archaic paradigm that is no longer useful. It's not unusual to hear a "notable silence—caused by a string of unfilled appointments" (McKibben, 2016) at many schools. Some family members don't have the time or transportation to attend conferences. It's not a matter of not caring about their child's schooling—of course they do. Often, it's the reality of availability and logistics.

Some family members might be used to the dreaded "phone call home." Unfortunately, calling home is often the tool used to convey the child's transgressions. In contrast, a positive phone call home can "contribute to building trust, rapport, and community" (Albert, 2017) in your classroom. Begin the year with a positive phone call home; introduce yourself, the purpose of your class, and some topics your students will be learning.

Think of the various ways you communicate with family members: phone calls, e-mails, text messages, or educational apps. With all of that communication going on, it's surprising there could ever be miscommunication, but it does happen.

PREVENT MISCOMMUNICATION

Preprinted Postcards

Give each student several preprinted postcards at the beginning of the year. Ask students to write their addresses on each postcard. Then, when you want to share good news, jot down a few lines, and send it in the mail. This takes little time on your part because the postcard is ready to go. Students will feel grateful knowing their hard work is being shared with their family. (See figure 6.1.)

Rationale: This brief communication with family members can quickly establish positive relationships right away at the start of the school year. Within the first week, send a postcard home sharing good news about a child's attendance or warm disposition or attentiveness to organization. Find something in which to compliment and commend.

Student Newsletter

Put a spin on the traditional student newsletter by having students write the newsletter. Give students chances to upload pictures, draw cartoons, or write articles of interest. Students will feel proud communicating their classroom news with their families.

Rationale: The student newsletter, while an important communication tool, can also be considered a learning tool. Students have the opportunity to create a newspaper—complete with editors, cartoonists, investigative reporters, and feature writers. Creating a newsletter could be the chance to showcase their writing skills, artistic talents, leadership capabilities, or innate inquisitiveness.

(Front)

```
┌─────────────────────────────────────────────────────────┐
│                                              [Stamp]    │
│  School's Address                                       │
│                                                         │
│                   **Student Writes His Address**        │
│                                                         │
│                                                         │
└─────────────────────────────────────────────────────────┘
```

(Back)

```
┌─────────────────────────────────────────────────────────┐
│  Today's Date                                           │
│  Dear _____:                         │
│  Hello! I just wanted to take this opportunity to share │
│  good news with you regarding today's                   │
│  class/Check-Up/discussion.                             │
│  Please take this opportunity to ask _____ about │
│  the work that is being done in our class.              │
│  Thank you,                                             │
│  Mrs. Grafwallner                                       │
│  Phone Number                                           │
└─────────────────────────────────────────────────────────┘
```

Figure 6.1.   Example of a Preprinted Postcard

Student Teaching

At the beginning of the year, create a calendar where two or three students per month "teach" lessons of what they have learned that month in an evening performance. If it's an English class, perhaps students will lead a critical-thinking discussion, or if it is a science class, perhaps students will demonstrate a lab. Give students the chance to showcase the important work they do and the crucial learning that goes on in their classroom.

Rationale: Teaching is the ultimate understanding. Giving students a chance to demonstrate their learning to a family audience, perhaps even a grandparent, helps to grow their confidence, contemplation, and contentment. Students can teach a lesson they feel particularly knowledgeable about, devising their own lesson plans and critical-thinking questions for intriguing discussion.

Collaborative Conference Log

During a parent–teacher conference or some other family meeting, complete the collaborative conference log (see figure 6.2) with the family member and student. Determine what's working in class, and discuss a challenge the student can focus on. Then complete the chart, assigning everyone a role that can support the student in progressing past his challenge.

Rationale: The collaborative conference log is a progress tool that gives all stakeholders the opportunity to create a supportive, responsible partnership. Teachers, family members, and students take part in authentic conversation that is meant to differentiate roles and give everyone a chance to work toward a common purpose. In addition, students can practice how to take the lead position in their education—learning how to identify what they need and communicating how to get there.

Dear Family Letter

At the end of each quarter, assign a "Dear Family" letter (see textbox 6.1). As part of each quarter reflection, ask students to write a letter to a family member. Encourage them to share the content of the class, their participation in class, the relevance of the class, and their feelings toward the class.

Dear Family Letter

Gives students the opportunity to share their school day and, more specifically, the valuable work they are doing in school with their family members.

Dear Family,
I am excited to tell you about some of the things I have done during this quarter with Mr./Ms. [teacher's name].

First, I defined/listed/practiced _____.
Then, I explained/interpreted/summarized _____.
Next, I analyzed/measured/debated _____.
Finally, I created/modified/constructed _____.

Name of Student/Family: _____

Share the Mission / Vision / Philosophy / Motto of Your School or Class:

_____

What's working?	What are the challenges?
Student's next steps:	Teacher's next steps:
Parent's next steps:	Follow-up: e-mail / phone call / meeting

Figure 6.2. Collaborative Conference Log

As I continue in this class, I want to continue to improve. Some ways I will continue to show progress are _____.

In closing, thank you for reading my letter. I hope you enjoyed learning more about [name of class].

Sincerely,

Rationale: The "Dear Family" letter encourages dialogue between students and family members that goes beyond the typical after-school conversation of "How was school today?" or "What did you learn in school today?" Giving students structured class time to comment on the topics of study, the discussions, or the assignments from the past quarter might help home conversations be more illuminating and interesting.

FAMILY AS RESOURCE

Some family members may have had negative experiences when they were in school. Perhaps they remember a teacher who was disrespectful or students who were aggressive or a school that seemed disinterested in them. We know that many "educators are doing many things that are not in the education experiences of parents" when they were going to school (Whitby, 2014), such as creating more student-centered opportunities, offering more learning choices, or encouraging diverse conversations about self and community. For some family members, these negative feelings have prohibited them from being strong school advocates. You have the opportunity to turn that mindset around. Establishing a positive culture with parents immediately gives you a chance to demonstrate to them their important role in their children's education and what they can bring to their children's academic success.

Family members are a school's best resource. They have intimate insights into their children's successes and challenges; in addition, they bring valuable interests, hobbies, and pursuits that schools can use to strengthen student engagement and motivation. It is important to tap into this vital resource and show students that their family members are equal partners in their education. The following suggestions show parents how to be an integral part of the classroom community.

Family Survey

At the beginning of the year, distribute the family survey (see textbox 6.2). This survey is meant as a way to get to know your students from the family's point of view. Family members can share background knowledge to help the teacher create personalized and engaging lessons.

Family Survey

Keeps teachers and families connected and can be used to design personalized lessons for students.

The typical interest inventory is given by teachers to students to learn more about them. But what about an interest inventory given by the teacher to family members to learn more about their children? To create a true partnership with parents, it is vital to acknowledge the expertise of the family members and their insightful knowledge of their own children. Teachers can apply their knowledge to create engaging, motivating, and personalized lessons to move their children forward!

Personal

1. What is your child's/family's favorite activity? (This can be a hobby, game, outing with friends, etc.) Can you tell me more about it?
2. What is your child's least favorite activity? (This can be a hobby, game, anything that your child does not like to do or attend.) Can you tell me why?
3. How many siblings does your child have? What are their names and ages?
4. Is your child involved in any extracurricular activities (school-based, club, or neighborhood)?
5. Is your child in any type of leadership position? (e.g., Boy Scouts, neighborhood club, sports club captain)
6. Does your family/your child have a pet? If so, what kind, and what is its name?
7. Is there something that triggers your child to become emotional or upset?
8. Does your child have access to the internet at home?
9. What motivates your child?
10. What words best describe your child's character?

Academics

1. What is your child's favorite school subject?
2. What is your child's least favorite school subject?

3. What motivates your child to do their best work?
4. What are your child's strengths at school?
5. Has your child ever had a difficult experience (e.g., academically, socially, emotionally) in school? If so, could you please explain the circumstances?
6. If your child wasn't in school, what would he/she be doing instead?
7. What does your child miss the most about his class/teacher from last year?
8. Does your child work best alone, with a partner, or in a group?
9. How does your child learn best?
10. Is there anything that you would like me to know about your child?

Rationale: Typically, students complete an interest inventory so teachers can learn more about them and to create personalized learning. But sending home a family survey is an opportunity to learn special details that can be transferred to the classroom to create an academic family.

This Century

Distribute the "This Century" form (see figures 6.3 and 6.4) to students, and ask them to give it to a family member who lived through an iconic or significant time in history. Then, invite the family members to school to share their stories with the class.

This project is interesting and accessible and demonstrates universal design. Students in any grade level and at any ability level can readily participate. Because the directions are open-ended, a "significant historical event" can be what the student wants it to be. For example, Max, a student, chose to give his forms to his Great Aunt Joan and his Uncle Jim. Aunt Joan wrote about the rations during World War II, while Uncle Jim wrote about the first American astronaut in space. However, the directions didn't prevent another student from writing about a different event that he and his family considered significant or historical.

This particular project gives family members and children a chance to share meaningful historical events in a way that history books cannot replicate. Max was especially excited about his Uncle Jim's response simply

This Century

Month _____ Year _____

Written by guest columnist Joan A. Janiszewski (Great Aunt Joan)

I Remember When ...

World War II began and all the sacrifices the American people made to ensure a victory for the Allies.

I was only ten years old at the time, and I had a brother in the navy who was at Pearl Harbor at the time of the Japanese attack. His ship, a destroyer, had pulled into the bay for repairs, and his crew was spending several days aboard other ships while this was taking place. Fortunately for him, his ship was not a direct hit. But he was involved in all the panic that took place that Sunday morning.

We at home had all of our food, gas, and shoes rationed. We could not buy a new car, stove, refrigerator, washing machine, etc. because all the materials used to manufacture these items went into making airplanes, ships, tanks, etc. for the war effort.

We were all happy and relieved when the war ended and our servicemen came home, and we could begin to buy new cars and items for our homes again.

Figure 6.3. "This Century" by Great Aunt Joan

because, as a 10-year-old boy, he considered space travel adventurous, courageous, and dangerous.

Think about this project as an opportunity for familial conversation that transcends the ordinary "I remember when" because it's not something that happened to someone else; rather, it's an experience, a memory, or a situation that happened to them or their family. In that way, it's far more relevant, relative, and refreshing!

Rationale: The "This Century" form gives family members the opportunity to highlight a historical event from their perspective. This special look at living history helps students to see events from differing viewpoints. Students have the chance to ask questions, form ideas, and develop research questions based on these unique, historical perspectives.

A Picture Is Worth a Thousand Words

Ask students to locate vintage pictures of their community from various websites. For instance, check a local historical society, such as the Milwaukee County Historical Society (https://milwaukeehistory.net); a local public museum, such as the Milwaukee Public Museum (https://www.mpm.edu/research-collections/photographs); or the Smithsonian Institution Archives (https://siarchives.si.edu/what-we-do/photograph-and-image-collections). In-

This Century

Month _____ Year _____

Written by guest columnist Jim Meyer (Uncle Jim)

I Remember When . . .

It was May 1961, and we were huddled in front of a small black and white TV watching intently. There had been many delays, caused by broken parts in the rocket ship that stood by itself in the middle of a large open field. The TV announcer kept trying to fill time by repeating what was going on. All three networks—NBC, CBS, and ABC—were providing coverage.

Finally, after hours of waiting, we heard the words coming from the TV: "10, 9, 8, 7, 6, 5, 4, 3, 2, 1—Ignition. Liftoff."

I remember my mom and dad applauding the rocket as it slowly lifted off the launch pad on top of a bright, white-hot flame.

Alan Shepard, America's first astronaut, was on the first American rocket (a Redstone) inside a Mercury space capsule. It was a tiny thing, smaller than a phone booth, but it represented our country's first entry into space.

I was nine years old, and I knew from that day on I wanted to be an astronaut. As time goes by, we sometimes realize our dreams don't always come true, but if NASA came to me today and asked if I wanted to go into space, I would say "YES!"

Figure 6.4. "This Century" by Uncle Jim

vite neighborhood senior citizens to share their memories. How has their community changed? How has it stayed the same? How do the changes and similarities influence the community today?

Rationale: Neighborhood senior citizens can offer a glimpse into the transformations of a community. Many of these neighbors have lived in the community all of their lives; as a result, they can share memories of the way the neighborhood used to be and what it is today. In addition, they can share how those changes affected the citizens of that community and what those changes mean to society today. Students have the opportunity to ask questions and learn more about their local neighborhood history.

Neighborhood Community Leader

Ask students to interview a community leader: the local police chief, a restaurant chef, or a local store owner. How does the community leader form positive relationships with neighbors? How do they give back to the community? What is one recommendation they have to make the community a better place?

Rationale: Community leaders have a significant responsibility—creating a neighborhood that is safe, responsible, and respectful. Students can learn the duties of these community leaders and voice their optimism and concerns about their neighborhoods. In addition, students can offer suggestions on how to make their neighborhoods more positive, welcoming places for all residents.

My Favorite Food

Invite family members to cook their favorite food for the class. While sharing the food, share the story behind it. Are the ingredients indicative of a certain geographical area? Are there cultural legends or traditions about the food? Why is the food important to your family?

Rationale: Family members have a chance to share their traditions, cultures, and ethnicities with students through food. Family members can share the history behind the recipes, the specific ingredients, and the social satisfaction that food brings to those who share it. Students have the opportunity to ask questions and gain valuable insights into the cultures and traditions of these recipes. Also, students can try preparing the recipe at home and share reviews with the class.

CONCLUSION

Family members are crucial to the success of education, and for far too long, they have remained on the fringe of academics. The partnership of student, family, and teacher cannot be undervalued. In the elementary grades, it is common to see family members in school, listening to students read or helping the teacher with secretarial tasks. But it seems that, in the middle and high school classrooms, family members are absent. While family members attend traditional school events, such as parent–teacher conferences or athletic banquets, few family members are seen in classrooms. One reason may be the embarrassment students might feel with family members present, or family members may think that their presence is no longer necessary or warranted. However, remind family members that they are always welcome and embraced in your classroom. Their life experiences can be a valued living history lesson, and their willingness to help with mundane secretarial tasks is certainly appreciated. Family members want to support teachers—show them how.

HOW TO USE CHAPTER 6

Book Study Reflection Questions

1. How do you introduce yourself to family members? Share your method with your colleagues.
2. How do you communicate with family members? Share your suggestions with your colleagues.
3. Choose one of the communication ideas from this chapter to implement. Why did you choose this method? Share your reflections.
4. How do you use family members as resources? Share your suggestions with your colleagues.
5. Brainstorm ways to support families in their children's learning. Share your suggestions with your colleagues.

Professional Learning Community Discussion Questions

1. How does your department introduce itself to family members? Write your methods on a piece of poster paper, and share with other departments; demonstrate, if possible.
2. How does your department communicate with family members? Write your methods of communication on a piece of poster paper, and share with other departments; demonstrate, if possible.
3. How does your department use families as resources? Create a list on a piece of poster paper, and share with other departments; demonstrate, if possible.
4. If the communication between department and family members is not positive, how does your department work to overcome that negative relationship?

Professional Development Discussion Questions

1. As the teacher leader, how do you introduce yourself, your school, and its mission and vision to family members?
2. How do you positively communicate with family members? Share your methods with the staff.
3. How do you mediate between teachers and family members when the relationship is problematic?

4. How do you encourage family members to give their talents to your school? Offer suggestions to your staff.

Chapter Seven

Change Your Language, Change Your Mind-set

Education is cyclical—things that were once old are later new again. Think about the typical jargon used in education: What was once "writing the test first" is now eloquently labeled "backward design." What was once "teaching to various learning styles" is now referred to as "differentiation." What was once described as "tinkering" is now labeled "21st-century skills," and the term *digital natives* (termed by Mark Prensky in 2001) is now considered passé. Regardless of language shifts, the goal remains the same: support and assist students in becoming the best citizens, curious learners, and extraordinary thinkers they can be.

Now imagine being a parent and trying to navigate through the tidal wave of educational language. It can be confusing and discouraging. When talking with parents, be aware of the language you're using, especially if you are peppering your conversation with the latest buzzwords, research catchphrases, or subject-specific acronyms. Make sure you use them sparingly, and define each one. While buzzwords, catchphrases, and acronyms serve a purpose and aid teachers in communicating with each other, certain words can also build a divide between parents and teachers. The use of academic language can be exclusionary; therefore, refrain from using language that might cause divisiveness with parents. You want to use language that inspires and motivates parents because your words are often the link between school and home.

The following words should be omitted; use their suggested replacements instead.

SAY *DEVELOPING* INSTEAD OF *STRUGGLING* OR *RELUCTANT*

As you communicate with parents, imagine being on the receiving end of that conversation. How would you want the information to be delivered and received? Often, educators use the terms *struggling* or *reluctant* when referring to student learning. These terms cannot be allowed to reference learners who need your support. These terms come from a deficit model of thinking that, somehow, some students will never become the learners you want them to be; rather, they will continually fail according to some district-initiated benchmark or criteria.

According to Merriam-Webster's (n.d.) online dictionary, the term *struggling* means "to proceed with difficulty or with great effort," and *reluctant* means "feeling or showing aversion, hesitation, or unwillingness." Imagine using those words during a parent–teacher conference. Or envision showing these definitions to a student and using these words when referring to their learning—or lack of it? Of course, the parent would be shocked and discouraged, and the student would feel disgruntled and frustrated.

Let's modify these terms to *developing* because all of us are developing at something. We simply are not there *yet*. Imagine being labeled a "struggling" learner: No matter how hard one tries, no matter the small bursts of progress, the label would become so ingrained in that individual that it could actually *define* her. Now imagine explaining to a student that she is a "developing" learner. According to Merriam-Webster's (n.d.) online dictionary, *developing* means "to acquire gradually." That's a definition a student can live with and grow into. It means we can work together for a successful outcome. So the next time you're tempted to refer to a student as *struggling* or *reluctant*, consider eliminating that deficit thinking; instead, replace these with the word *developing*. In that way, all students will have a chance to proceed, progress, and promote!

SAY *GOALS* INSTEAD OF *GRADES*

Grades are important to parents and students. To some degree, they define student learning. But grades are asked to cover a lot of ground about what students are supposed to know and be able to do. It's nearly impossible to "combine aspects of students' achievement, attitude, responsibility, effort, and behavior into a single grade that's recorded on a report card" (Guskey, 2011, p. 19), yet that's what teachers are expected to do. Perhaps it's time to question not only the fundamental meaning of grades but also the word itself. Instead of using the traditional language associated with the word *grade*, think of also adding the world *goal*.

The definition of *goal* is the "result or achievement toward which effort is directed" (Dictionary.com, n.d.). Apply that definition when explaining to parents that their children's achievement has been directed toward a specific outcome. For example, as students revise their rough drafts in English class, you could share that the student's goal has been to write analysis with more clarity and precision.

To make the connection energizing and practical, give students the opportunity to write their own goals. What specifically does the student want to accomplish? Distribute the student goal-setting template (figure 7.1), and give students time to practice goal setting. Also, give students the chance to add verbs and outcomes to the template so they can truly take responsibility for and ownership of their own learning. This type of responsibility propels students toward success. When you help students to focus on goals, you concentrate on more than just numbers or percentages or averages. Goals give students the chance to focus on the process of progress.

Consider having students create a goals template based on four core concepts: academic, personal, behavioral, and global. What do they want to accomplish academically? Maybe, for one student, it is earning an A on a challenging checkup; perhaps, for another student, an academic goal is to raise her hand in class and participate more. What do your students want to accomplish personally? Perhaps one student wants to focus on getting to his job on time regularly, while another student's goal is to cut down on the junk food she eats and replace it with fresh fruit. What do your students want to accomplish behaviorally? Maybe one student's goal is to be kinder to his younger siblings, while another student wants to focus on limiting his salty language. What do your students want to accomplish globally? Perhaps a few students want to work on a plan to cut down on the trash in the cafeteria and have made it their mission to instill a compost program at school, while another student wants to be more cognizant of what is happening in the world around him and has decided to listen to NPR or the BBC more often to stay up to date. Goals do not have to be intensely overwhelming. Assist students in creating goals that they can actually accomplish so they can see progress. Often, goals are so lofty and overzealous that they cannot be kept. Assist your students in creating goals that are doable and enjoyable.

Component	Questions	Verbs	Me
Specific	What exactly do you want to **accomplish**? What is the **purpose** or benefits of your goal?	Research Write Investigate Study Explore Create Generate Produce Analyze Build Implement Apply Utilize Employ	I want to . . . Because . . .
Measurable	How will you **measure your progress** and success?	Demonstrate Study Prepare Organize Arrange Model Show Teach Express Perform	I will measure progress/success because I will be able to . . .
Attainable	Do you have **sufficient time** to accomplish your goal? What other types of **resources** do you need to attain your goal?	Offer Complete by date/quarter/semester	I will show progress/success by . . . Some things standing in my way could be . . .
Relevant	Why is it **significant**?		This goal is significant because . . .
Timely	When will this **goal be achieved**?		I will achieve my goal by . . .

Figure 7.1. Student Goal-Setting Template

Replacing *grades* with *goals* does not have to be an either/or proposition. Instead, consider marrying the two to demonstrate that, while grades offer a picture of student knowledge, goals makes that picture meaningful and personal.

SAY *VIGOR* INSTEAD OF *RIGOR*

The debate has long raged about the use of the word *rigor*. For some parents, *rigor* is identified with getting into the right high school and the right college. Parents feel a sense of pride when they read that their children's school has a "rigorous" curriculum or the homework and assessments are "rigorous." Yet, other parents might see *rigor* as a negative, assuming that too much rigor is too much pressure for students to bear. In addition, students might feel that a rigorous curriculum is out of their reach—it is simply too hard for them to accomplish. Increasing rigor does not mean more and longer homework assignments; rather, it means time and opportunity for students to develop and apply habits of mind as they navigate sophisticated and reflective learning experiences.

Rigor comes from the Latin phrase "rigor mortis": *Rigor* means "stiffness," and *mortis* means "of death." Another definition of *rigor* by Blackburn (2013) is in "creating an environment in which each student is expected to learn at high levels, each student is supported so he or she can learn at high levels, and each student demonstrates learning at high levels" (p. 10). Instead of creating lessons of rigor, why not create lessons of vigor? Lessons of vigor encompass three distinct thinking components—thinking critically, thinking creatively, and thinking flexibly—thereby creating classrooms that are stimulating, engaging, and supportive.

A Thinking Critically Classroom

A thinking critically classroom is one where process is the key to learning. While the final product is important, do not overlook the process. To create a thinking critically classroom, focus on conceptualizing, applying, analyzing, synthesizing, and evaluating the information students are taught. For example, in a high school humanities classroom, students might be reading the Gettysburg Address. After annotating the address, ask students to analyze the address based on how it affected our country emotionally, financially, and culturally. Then, evaluate that information and determine how those outcomes affect our country today.

When your students are able to think beyond the essentials of defining, listing, locating, and explaining, they can truly interact with the text and its meaning. They are learning to think critically and are able to achieve based on their thinking.

A Thinking Creatively Classroom

A thinking creatively classroom encourages choices and allows mistakes. However, consider limiting the choices offered so students are not beleaguered with the choice itself but rather are able to make solid selections based on what they know about themselves as learners. For example, when teaching note taking, give students three different templates from which to choose. Then, students can pick the template that works best for them. In addition, give students opportunities to fail and learn from the failure.

If a student happens to fail a checkup, schedule a one-on-one conference and have the student explain the failure. Did the student fail the checkup because she didn't have time or make time to study, because she didn't know how to prepare, or because she didn't understand the questions? When talking with the student, try to determine the source of her failure, and then ask the student how she plans to try again. What would work for her to be successful? What can she learn from the failure that would support her in trying again? Chances to reabsorb, rewrite, react, reengineer, and reengage have to be encouraged and offered.

Whatever the activity (composing a song, writing an essay, organizing a party, etc.), it is more likely to be a personal success if the creator focuses on and enjoys the activity in and of itself and doesn't worry about what other people may say or think. Therefore, give your students the opportunity to be creative without assessment. Let them choose, and let them change.

A Thinking Flexibly Classroom

In a thinking flexibly classroom, students are encouraged to look at problems and solve them in unique ways. One problem-solving technique is not enough in our 21st-century world. Students need to put on a different thinking cap to stretch beyond what they know. For example, imagine being in an 11th-grade environmental science class. Students are put in groups of three. Their task: Create a plan to ban plastics in their school. Just putting up signs demanding students to stop using plastic isn't enough. Students have to be able to think flexibly to create a sustainable, meaningful, and student-friendly plastics-ban strategy.

Students need to be taught how to use different thinking caps for various situations and experiences. In a thinking flexibly classroom, the learning experience motivates students to question their assumptions and think deeper. Students feel a sense of personal accomplishment when they are able to engage their personal intellects and challenge or change their preconceived notions.

SAY *CHECKUP* INSTEAD OF *TEST, QUIZ,* OR *ASSESSMENT*

For some students and their parents, test anxiety is real, and their concern is palpable. Students wake up with an upset stomach, and worried parents try to cajole their children to attend school—knowing that the cause of the malady isn't a virus but rather a test. As a result, it is important to demonstrate empathy and to show students that you understand their trepidation. Instead of using the traditional and worrisome language of *test* or *quiz*, change your language to reflect what you really want—an awareness of your students' understanding or comprehension of a text, piece of art, or refrain of music.

During test-taking situations, do not allow the words *test* or *quiz* to be used; they are words associated with evaluation. Sometimes when taking a test, there is no recourse or do-over. The grade is the grade—it is all but etched in stone. If the grade is poor, then the student failed, and the entire experience is considered a failure. However, a checkup determines if students can synthesize their learning. If they can't synthesize their learning, then you can find out the reason. What can you and the students do differently to be successful on the next checkup? A checkup tells the student that she has the opportunity to try again because this is a snapshot of her learning *at this time*. This change of language can alleviate most of your students' and their parents' concerns and fears. In addition, because it is a checkup, feedback is expected and anticipated. Students will be eager to learn how they can better prepare for the next checkup to demonstrate their understanding.

CONCLUSION

Eliminating doubtful language can help you create a more community-centered classroom, a less anxiety-ridden student, and a more knowledgeable parent. Your students will appreciate your sensitivity and compassion for their personal and academic lives, their parents will appreciate a more partnership-like approach, and you will appreciate a more energized and self-confident classroom.

HOW TO USE CHAPTER 7

Book Study Reflection Questions

1. Give examples of language you use in your class that support and engage your students. How does that language help your students to be more successful in your classroom?
2. How have you created a thinking critically classroom? Offer examples to your colleagues.
3. How have you created a thinking creatively classroom? Offer examples to your colleagues.
4. How have you created a thinking flexibly classroom? Offer examples to your colleagues.

Professional Learning Community Discussion Questions

1. Within your department, share how you have changed or revised the language in your classrooms to reflect a progressive mind-set.
2. Within your department, give an example of a lesson that has thinking critically components. Ask your department members for glows and grows feedback.
3. Within your department, give an example of a lesson that has thinking creatively components. Ask your department members for glows and grows feedback.
4. Within your department, give an example of a lesson that has thinking flexibly components. Ask your department members for glows and grows feedback.

Professional Development Discussion Questions

1. As the teacher leader, what language do you use when speaking with parents? Share your language with your colleagues.
2. As the teacher leader, demonstrate how you have created a thinking critically school. Encourage your colleagues to offer glows and grows.
3. As the teacher leader, demonstrate how you have created a thinking creatively school. Encourage your colleagues to offer glows and grows.

4. As the teacher leader, demonstrate how you have created a thinking flexibly school. Encourage your colleagues to offer glows and grows.

Chapter Eight

Share What You've Learned with Others

Sharing resources and strategies advances students' learning. Special education teachers are experts in the philosophy and practice of differentiation. They don't simply do differentiation—they employ it as a mind-set needed to teach well. Demonstrating for one student how to apply a strategy benefits all students. To be a truly gifted teacher, it is vital to offer classroom support and to ask for it, as well. In sharing what you've learned with colleagues, you demonstrate your desire to support them and their work. In addition, sharing lesson suggestions or pedagogical theory shows that you are thinking beyond you and your colleagues to what the students need to be successful. The following four resources can be used in all content areas and with all abilities.

RESOURCE 1: QUESTION-ANSWER RELATIONSHIP (QAR)

One strategy that supports students across all content areas and in all abilities is Dr. Taffy Raphael's iconic question-answer relationship (QAR) comprehension strategy. QAR provides a framework for organizing questioning activities and comprehension instruction. For most of a student's academic career, the teacher has asked the questions. As a result, students often find it difficult to manage complex text because a majority of their learning has been built around answering questions and not *creating* questions about topics in which they have an interest. However, teaching students how to ask questions and to build research questions from basic inquiry demonstrates a hierarchy of learning.

When introducing this strategy, offer students sentence stems to defuse any concern or trepidation about them having to create questions on their own. The stems provide a safety net of universal design so students are able to show what they know. Give students a piece of text. Teach the skill of annotation to students (see chapter 1). Then, distribute the QAR graphic organizer (see figure 8.1). As students review their annotated texts, ask them to answer different kinds of questions. The following are the questions to ask for *Goldilocks and the Three Bears*.

Who, What, Where, and When Questions

These are based on the text, where the answers can be found "right there" within the text.

Why and How Questions

These are based on inferences, where the answers have to be surmised or inferred based on the text.

Research Questions

For these, students create a series of questions based on more information they want to know about the subject. You can give your students examples of questioning techniques, so eventually they will be the ones asking the questions and facilitating the discussion. Eventually, they will be in charge of their own learning—a higher-level skill, absolutely.

RESOURCE 2: PICTURE BOOKS

Using picture books in all classrooms is one way to bridge the language gap. English-language learners (ELL) and developing readers can use picture books to share their knowledge, interests, and curiosity. One might think of picture books for bedtime, but picture books can be used in all classrooms, in all content areas, and with students of all abilities.

While printed text is important, if readers only focus on written text, then teachers and students miss out on a rich visual-learning experience. Serafini (2011) contends that picture books are multimodal examples that convey

"Right There" Questions (Who, What Where, and When)
1. Who is. . . ? Who was. . . ?
2. What is the. . . ? What has the. . . ? What can. . . ?
3. Where does. . . ? Where did. . . ?
4. When is the. . . ? When did the. . . ? When does the. . . ?
"Think and Search" Questions (Why and How: Inference)
1. Why do you think. . . ?
2. Why did he. . . ?
3. How does she/he feel toward. . . ? How do you know?
4. How does the relationship. . . ?
5. How can he. . . ?
6. How does society interact when. . . ?
"On Your Own/Further Research" Questions
I am interested in learning more about:

Figure 8.1. Question-Answer Relationship (QAR) Strategy Courtesy of Taffy Raphael and Peg Grafwallner

meaning in a variety of ways: written narratives, visual images, and design elements. Students have the opportunity to use any one of these examples or a combination of them to make meaning that they understand and that they can convey to their peers.

In the English/language arts classroom or during the World War II unit in history, consider showing the picture book *I Never Saw Another Butterfly: Children's Drawings and Poems from the Terezin Concentration Camp, 1942–1944* (Volavokova, 1994). Students who have little background on the

Holocaust or the ravages of World War II are able to infer the horrors of war based on the pictures in the book. Consider using the QAR graphic organizer as students page through the picture book. Their questions might be considerably different than questions based on written text.

For middle school music appreciation, consider using picture books of musicians during the first week of class. For instance, the picture book *Jimi: Sounds Like a Rainbow: A Story of the Young Jimi Hendrix* (Golio & Steptoe, 2010) can introduce a musician and a genre of music that students might not be familiar with. As students read the books and look at the pictures, ask them to reflect on the narrative, images, and design elements of the book. What are the main ideas of the book? What do the images tell us about Jimi Hendrix? What design elements (line, shape, color) help tell the story of Jimi Hendrix? Picture books can assist students in discussing major concepts where they may have insufficient background.

RESOURCE 3: CLASSROOM TALK

Student conversations are vital in building and nurturing imaginations, relationships, and self-regulation. Structured student conversations lend themselves to inquiry and wonder and demonstrate to students how to use talk to facilitate discussions of learning. First, it is important to get the classroom talking. Consider using the "What Do I Already Know?" form (figure 5.1) as a way to build engagement. Ask a student to facilitate the discussion by calling on members of the class. Ask another student to write down student responses as they share what they know about a particular topic. You can jot down the names of students who remain silent and determine how to support them in this new topic.

Next, model your thinking out loud as the lesson unfolds. Give students a pack of sticky notes, and as you demonstrate solving the problem or creating the lab, encourage your students to write down their questions to capture their thinking. Then give your students time to talk to each other as they inquire and wonder about the problem or lab based on their sticky notes.

Equally important is to listen carefully and sincerely as students share their thoughts and opinions. Creating a safe, judgment-free atmosphere encourages students to share their beliefs and feelings. Providing them the opportunity to guide the conversation encourages them to participate. Also, urging students to ask questions about how a peer came to her thoughts or ideas turns the attention to the process and shows students that what they are doing is indeed important work. Their use of inquiry (use the QAR as a guide) illustrates their critical-thinking skills and their curiosity.

Finally, by creating a classroom of conversationalists, students are developing interest, independence, and imagination, thereby becoming a classroom of strategic thinkers. Language is powerful and influential and ought to be considered as important as the reading and writing component of literacy. However, strategic conversation is often overlooked and sometimes misconstrued as a classroom management issue. Therefore, it is crucial to focus on talk and the power it can bring to the classroom.

RESOURCE 4: MULTIMEDIA TO SUPPORT VOCABULARY LEARNING

Today, students rely on the internet for everything they need: topics of interest, questions they need answered, or something as ordinary as homework help. Using the internet for vocabulary learning can turn a tedious lesson into a multimodal learning opportunity. Learning vocabulary should involve numerous authentic opportunities for students, such as in their own oral and written language. Therefore, vocabulary and technology together are a logical and artistic fit.

Students can create brief, stimulating videos depicting vocabulary words to study. For example, students could video themselves using a vocabulary word in conversation or create skits where the vocabulary word is used. Many students will enjoy the process and embrace the innovative way to learn the words. Encouraging students to share their videos with others helps students to remember the target words and associate the target words with various synonyms.

Also, there are many online tools, such as Quizlet (https://quizlet.com), Vocabulary.com (https://www.vocabulary.com), and Funbrain (for ESL learners; https://www.funbrain.com/games), to help students study vocabulary in creative and interesting ways. Due to the motivating and meaningful lessons, students are able to take responsibility for their vocabulary acquisition and are more apt to use what they have learned, not only in class, but in their social lives, as well.

Twitter, blogs, and multimodal word webs are just a few examples of what students can do to make vocabulary learning authentic. You can use these examples of multimodal learning to assist students in learning the way that best works for them. While some students may appreciate the timeless lecture, some students might welcome the freedom to use their skills to show what they know and how they can teach others. Allowing and encouraging a multimodal classroom not only aids the students in different ways of learning, but it also benefits the teacher in creating an inventive and exciting classroom to share with their colleagues.

TEACHER ABILITIES

As you share resources, strategies, and lessons with your colleagues, consider also how to share your talents of writing, presenting, and networking with other educators. They can learn much from the valuable work you do.

Publish

If you think you have nothing to say, know that you do. As an expert in your classroom, you can share the academic strategies and behavioral interventions you use every day. Even if you don't consider yourself a writer, take time to share your thoughts with others. Often you don't have to look any further than your own district to find a writing opportunity. Write a column for your school or district newsletter about a strategy or lesson you created, but remember your audience: parents and community members. Therefore, don't use teacher-ese, and keep the article practical.

Present

The idea of presenting to a crowd makes some people wince, but think of sharing what you've learned with a group of professionals who are always looking for new ideas and ways of learning. If you have a lesson plan that inspires and student artifacts that engage, share your work with other educators. Teachers want to know what their colleagues are doing; they want to be motivated and awed by what others are thinking and achieving. If you're not sure how to write a presentation proposal, check out local conference websites. Often it is a matter of completing an online form and submitting it. Also, take a look at various national conferences; they offer opportunities to share your passion nationwide.

Potential

When you think of your collegial potential, don't limit yourself to only those with whom you work. Networking is becoming increasingly more valuable in all professions—even education. When you pitch that article or submit that proposal, ask yourself how you can create a relationship—create personal potential—that will help you grow in your field.

Consider creating your own web page that shares your educational philosophy, your resumé, and your work. Use your web page as a platform to communicate best practices and innovative ideas that have worked in your classroom. Use social media as a way to grow your web page and expand your own repertoire of learning. Twitter, Facebook, LinkedIn, and Instagram promote education. EduChats are another way to build your professional network. Be drawn to a select few who have the same question you do: What can we learn from each other that will help us to support our students?

CONCLUSION

Sharing your work and your educational philosophy with other teachers supports your students' learning. Your willingness to share your work with other educators brings imaginative and inspirational lessons to teachers who are appreciative of your selflessness. Imparting your lessons to other teachers helps them in designing lessons that are more than just lecture: Interesting inquiry, picture books, classroom talk, and innovative vocabulary instruction are just some ways to help students think in creative and analytical ways.

In the world of education, marketing and networking has become increasingly important. Students must remain our focus; however, in this new age, it is crucial to market and network so the most knowledgeable educators continue to grow and motivate students. Publish and present to unleash your potential!

HOW TO USE CHAPTER 8

Book Study Reflection Questions

1. Offer an example of a resource or strategy you have shared with a teacher.

2. Discuss ways to encourage colleagues to share their resources or strategies if they are unwilling to do so.
3. Have you ever modified or revised a resource or strategy given to you by someone else? Explain how.
4. Explain how you have modified or scaffolded a lesson for all abilities.
5. Share your experiences of publishing, presenting, and networking. Has it been successful? Why? Why not?

Professional Learning Community Discussion Questions

1. Within your department, demonstrate how you have shared resources or strategies with other teachers.
2. Within your department, explain what you could do to encourage fellow department members to share their resources and strategies with others.
3. Within your department, demonstrate how you have modified or scaffolded lessons for all abilities.
4. Within your department, discuss ways in which department members could write a column for the parent newsletter, or create a professional development opportunity based on a department goal, or create potential academic communities with teachers from various schools or colleges.

Professional Development Discussion Questions

1. As the teacher leader, create ways in which teachers could observe their colleagues across content areas and share their resources.
2. As the teacher leader, connect teachers from various departments, and ask them to create cross-curricular strategies; for example, connect art to science, English to social studies, world languages to math, and so on. Ask those teachers to present their strategies at the next professional learning community meeting.
3. As the teacher leader, encourage teachers to share their scaffolded lessons showcasing how they modified for all abilities.
4. As the teacher leader, give teachers time to write for the parent newsletter, or create a workshop for the next professional learning community meeting. Set aside time for teachers to share their resources and strategies with the larger professional community.

Chapter Nine

Ask Your Colleagues for Help

You cannot do your job alone. You need your colleagues for support and your principal for guidance. One might think that asking for help shows weakness or an inability to do one's job. In contrast, asking for help demonstrates your willingness to learn and grow. Surround yourself with people of like mind to stay positive and progressive, prepared and practiced.

SUPPORTIVE COLLEAGUES

Building and sustaining relationships with colleagues is vital to the work you do and how you present that work to your students. Collaborating with peers can be one of the great joys of teaching. At the end of the workday, sharing your day's successes with your colleagues builds a common goal of accomplishment.

Likewise, commiserating about a failed lesson and lending an ear displays your willingness to listen. Offering suggestions and possible recommendations for next time shows your colleague that you are supportive in her desire to be a better teacher. However, while those hallway conversations are necessary to comradery, it is vital not to stay in that negative mind-set. It is easy to get sucked into the narrow-minded conversations that plague those who are unhappy. Be aware of the difference between processing and venting: Processing comes from a growth model, where the speaker wants to develop, reflect, and adjust. Processing is someone asking, "Could I just run this past you?" It's never a question of seeking approval or judgment. It's more of a thought process, a kind of "I've-thought-about-this-lesson-or-project-and-I-just-need-you-to-hear-if-there-are-any-kinks-in-my-idea." Often, giving the individual time to talk through an idea or a challenge leads to an answer or a chance to consider or reconsider.

In discussion, one will sometimes lament a classroom management issue, a poorly delivered lesson, or a difficult student. We all need to vent once in a while; it does a body good. However, instead of just wallowing in a "woe-is-me" mind-set, consider ways to remedy the challenges mentioned. You will know the teacher just needs a listening ear when she is open to your suggestions or ideas about how to make her classroom more engaging, more inspiring, and more inclusionary. If the venting teacher stays in that attitude, though, no amount of suggestions or assistance from you will help. The eruption might be about a tired district mandate or a foolish administrative rule or an irresponsible colleague. But nothing productive comes from the outburst, and the person who is venting is usually doing it for a selfish reason: She simply wants to dump her troubles on the listener.

It might be in your best interest to stay away from that viewpoint, but don't give up on that teacher completely. Continue to offer ideas and suggestions in e-mail and department or professional learning community meetings. Continue to help that teacher see that, while occasional venting is acceptable, staying in that negative mind-set is not.

METHOD OF PURPOSE

To create the most successful working atmosphere, it is important to design a method of purpose so those involved feel their time and talents have not been wasted. A teacher's day is not made up of meetings like a person in business. Teachers would rather spend their time with students. Therefore, it is imperative that meetings are productive.

It is not unusual for meetings to begin with several minutes of idle conversation as people get organized and prepared. While that is certainly one way to welcome participants, it can also lead to wasted time. A method of purpose maintains that the meeting has meaning and can begin when all are present. In that way, teachers know there will be a product or decision at the end of the meeting with key follow-up.

1. Begin with the End in Mind

When working with colleagues, decide the purpose of the collaboration. What is it that you want to do, share, or offer? Consider these possibilities:

- I want to assist my colleagues in learning how to _____.
- I want to support my colleagues in _____.
- I want to give my colleagues the opportunity to _____.

For example, "I will assist the members of the science department in learning how to use two-column note taking in their classrooms."

2. What Is the Purpose?

Giving your meeting purpose eliminates wasted time and wasted talent. You must be able to articulate the purpose of your meeting before you move on; otherwise, the outcome will be vague, and implementation could be disorganized:

- Will you design a lesson plan together?
- Will you create a professional development workshop?
- Will you outline an after-school tutoring session?

For example, "I will assist the biology teachers in modeling two-column note taking to students for an article about viruses."

3. What Are the Non-negotiables of the Purpose?

Without an articulation of the non-negotiables, you may feel your voice has gone unrecognized or some of your ideas weren't heard. Therefore, the non-negotiables give you the opportunity to share your particular expertise with the group:

- What are the two or three (you deem the number) most important outcomes?
- What two or three (you deem the number) concepts or questions or synthesizing must take place?

For example, "In designing a lesson plan using two-column note taking in the virus unit, it will be necessary that students create two-column notes using key words and details."

4. What Is Your Role?

When roles are clearly defined, all members know what they have to do for a successful outcome. If roles are not obvious, the work will not get done, or group members may feel that they were responsible for too much or not enough:

- Will you write the learning intention and the success criteria?
- Will you gather the resources?
- Will you collect the research?

For example, "I will model to the biology students how to take two-column notes using the chapter on viruses in their science books."

5. Stretch and Grow

It is easy to stay within one's comfort zone, but now is the time to stretch your thinking and experiences. If you have always volunteered to write the learning intention and the success criteria, now is the time to ask a colleague if he could help you find worthy research. What do you want to learn to become a better educator for the sake of your students?

For example, "I want to research various templates for two-column note taking so students have a choice of templates. Students can then choose the method that works best for them."

6. What Does Follow-up Look Like?

This meeting's work is vital to student growth and professional development. Therefore, it is important to support colleagues so they develop into knowledgeable and compassionate professional educators. If teachers don't envision themselves growing, their practice suffers, the relationships deteriorate, and the learning fails:

- How will we know if our purpose has been successful?
- How can we share (publish and present our potential) what we've learned with our colleagues?

- Do we need to meet again? If so, for what purpose?

For example, "During the modeling of the two-column notes, meeting members are invited to watch the demonstration and observe students. They are encouraged to take notes to share at follow-up. Then, student notes will be collected and brought to the meeting for members to review. Once reviewed, meeting members will provide suggestions and revisions and present this lesson design at an upcoming professional learning community meeting."

SUPPORTIVE COLLEAGUES AND COTEACHING

There are many models of coteaching: one teaches, one supports; team teaching; and parallel teaching, among others. However, all coteaching models are meant to provide students with the optimal learning environment. If you have not used a coteaching model, consider using the supportive-colleagues approach. The following is an example of coteaching with a classroom teacher, a special education teacher, and an instructional coach. This model can be revised and modified based on what you need, but the goal remains the same: How can you support your colleagues in creating engaging and motivating lessons to support student growth?

Up Close and Personal

Coteaching has become a buzzword in education but remains a nebulous term. Many educators or paraprofessionals refer to themselves as coteachers, but in truth, they merely stand on the sidelines, watching the classroom teacher teach. According to the Wisconsin Department of Public Instruction (2016), *coteaching* is "generally defined as two licensed educators, often a special education teacher and a general education teacher, sharing equal responsibility for planning, delivering, evaluating instruction, and learning to meet the diverse needs of students in a shared space." I have an equivalent licensure, with a #317 reading specialist license and a master's degree in education. Sometimes, I share instructional responsibility when I collaborate in creating lessons, but that's where it ends. I don't have accountability for a single group of students; I am not responsible for their grades.

But I consider myself highly responsible for their learning. During the year, I collaborate with our junior English teacher and special education teacher. The special education teacher is in the classroom, modifying, scaffolding, and revising lessons for student success. We meet when the classroom teacher is starting a new short story, novel, poem, drama, or writing opportunity. We begin by asking, "What is the purpose of the lesson, and what do we want our students to know and be able to do?" We share possibilities of skills, strategies, resources, and other ideas. Each of us has an equal, respected voice, deferring to our colleague's level of expertise.

Recently, the classroom teacher wanted a strategy that would engage students in asking different types of questions—some with specific answers, some open-ended. The special education teacher recommended question-answer relationship (QAR). I suggested two resources that scaffolded QAR. The first resource was the traditional QAR chart divided into three categories: "Right There," "Think and Search," and "Research." This particular graphic organizer could be offered to those students who feel confident in creating their own questions. The next resource I suggested was an adaptation of Doug Buehl's (2007) "Self-Questioning Taxonomy for Literature" to create a series of open-ended questions (see textbox 9.1). These open-ended questions aimed at assisting students in thinking more conceptually than linearly.

Open-Ended Questions
by Doug Buehl and Peg Grafwallner

Gives students the opportunity to reflect on questions for group work and guided thinking.

1. How have my background or experiences helped me to understand what the author is telling me?
2. Is my perspective, perception, or bias causing me to look at this text with a narrow lens?
3. Have my background or experiences influenced me in understanding this story or relating to it? If so, how?
4. How has my culture or ethnic background prohibited me from understanding this story or relating to it?
5. What does this story remind me of? Can I connect this story to something else I have read?
6. What lesson can I learn from what the author is telling me?
7. Does this lesson provide me with a cause to change (my mind, my bias, my perspective)? If so, how? If not, why not?

8. What am I supposed to understand from this story? Am I changed (personally, behaviorally, spiritually, emotionally, mentally) because of it?

We created a lesson based solely on student inquiry but scaffolded the lesson based on the students' abilities. We wanted students to see how they could transcend from generating basic recall questions to eventually creating questions.

Regarding the proximity to students, the special education teacher sat among the students, the classroom teacher stood in front of the room, and I stood in the back. Using the QAR form (see figure 8.1), the teacher asked students to generate one or more questions modeled after the question starters in each category. The special education teacher gathered several students and showed them how to use the question starters to create one of their own. The classroom teacher and I began moving around the room, listening to student conversation and encouraging students to continue their thinking.

The classroom teacher asked students for some key words from their conversations. As he called on students, I moved to the front of the class and began to write their key words on the whiteboard. The special education teacher offered words of encouragement to students to share their thoughts. She even convinced one student to write his key word on the board. The lesson continued with all of us weaving in and out of each other's sentences, checking student notes, and listening in to student conversations.

When the lesson was over, we debriefed. The classroom teacher felt this lesson successfully checked off his purpose and goal. He wanted students to use inquiry to create critical-thinking questions, realizing that some students might need assistance and support to create basic recall questions. We didn't focus on what students couldn't do; we concentrated on what they could do within their abilities. If you were to ask us if we cotaught the lesson, I am confident that all of us would say no, only because we don't necessarily see our relationship as coteachers but rather responding to the needs of our students and the respect toward each other's skills and knowledge. That respect translates to student success and empowerment in the classroom and beyond.

GUIDING PRINCIPAL

It is important to ask your principal for support. Don't assume she is too busy or not interested in your career. Truthfully, many principals are caught up in the day-to-day management tasks that are necessary to make a school and all of its components function well. When needing support, schedule a meeting with your principal. Create an outline of what you want to ask, suggest, or discuss prior to the meeting. Like your colleagues, your principal wants to know the goal of the meeting and what you want or need. Therefore, be upfront, truthful, and authentic in your outline. Create three or four thinking questions for your outline. For example, ask your principal where she sees you in five years; where does she see herself? How can your common vision align to create the best possible learning experience for students?

Up Close and Personal

When you do find that principal with whom you connect, it's best to listen, learn, and trust, as you absorb as much of their vision as you can. Principals look at the big picture and delegate ideas, suggestions, and concepts to the team. The strength of the vision should be in the trust that the work will be done. That trust becomes contagious, as all work together for the commonality of the vision.

The covenant is the promise within the mission and vision statement to colleagues, parents, and students that you will do what you say you are going to do and that you will be held accountable for the sake of the greater good. You will support colleagues so they develop into knowledgeable and compassionate professional educators. You will respect and communicate with parents to form partnerships that are enduring and trustworthy. Finally, you will create authentic opportunities for learning that give students the hope they deserve and the consideration they need. In short, the covenant keeps you and your colleagues working together to cultivate the best educational experience for peers, parents, and students.

When the covenant becomes too demanding or when the vision has not been made clear to all stakeholders, it is inevitable that the contract will become the purpose. If teachers don't envision themselves growing, if parents don't value the relationships, and if students become disengaged, our practice suffers, our relationships deteriorate, and our children fail. It is that simple. Standing up for the covenant begs the question, What do *you* stand for? When you are able to answer that confidently and with purpose, you are on your way to building a better school. Become a visionary who develops a confident team of teachers, a thankful legion of parents, and a considerate class of students.

CONCLUSION

Every experience is a learning opportunity. Method of purpose is designed to use time and talent to maximize the experience and expertise of colleagues. The supportive colleagues and coteaching model offers an opportunity to use the gifts of your colleagues to create inspirational learning opportunities for students.

Whether you are collaborating with colleagues, teacher leaders, or principals, asking for support is not a sign of weakness but an example of strength. Give yourself the chance to learn, and don't fear that asking for help is a mistake; to the contrary, it is a sure sign of wanting to do a job well.

HOW TO USE CHAPTER 9

Book Study Reflection Questions

1. How do you assist your colleagues who need your help?
2. How can you be a part of the method of purpose?
3. What is your definition of *coteaching*? Can you offer an example?
4. If you have never cotaught with a colleague, why not? If so, share how that looked.
5. How do you and your principal or teacher leader create opportunities for growth in your school?

Professional Learning Community Discussion Questions

1. With your department members, discuss how do you offer assistance to other department members?
2. With your department members, practice applying the method of purpose. Share its successes and challenges for your department with the faculty.
3. With your department members, demonstrate examples of coteaching.
4. With your department members, reach out to other departments and apply a coteaching model that works best for you.

Professional Development Discussion Questions

1. As the teacher leader, how do you ask for help and support from your faculty?
2. As the teacher leader, apply the method of purpose with other principals. Share its successes and challenges with your faculty and with the other schools involved.
3. As the teacher leader, offer to be a part of a coteaching plan with colleagues.
4. Share glows and grows with your faculty of your coteaching experience.

Chapter Ten

Celebrate—It's Good for the Soul

There are some days when laughter might be the last thing you're thinking of, but it may be just what you need. Your students come to you from different places—cognitively and logistically—yet a hearty chuckle or shared case of the giggles may help you and your students to take a step back and start again. While school is a serious business, it must also be a place of shared wonder and community. You must not let go of the commonalities that make your classroom an academic family full of purpose and passion. All families create opportunities to celebrate their joy. How will you create yours?

Classroom Advice (Middle School/High School). On the first day of school, before you distribute the syllabus, give your students a 3 × 5 notecard. Ask them to write down an important piece of advice (don't give too many directions—allow this to be organic) that they would tell someone upon entering the classroom. Collect the notecards and shuffle. Put students in small groups of three. Redistribute the cards. Ask students to determine which notecard is the one that is the best piece of advice. Circulate around the room. Once determined, ask a student to write down the advice on butcher block paper at the front of the classroom. Their advice will guide your classroom promise of respect.

Journal Promises (Middle School/High School). During the first week of school, distribute spiral notebooks to each student. Give students 15 minutes to respond to this first prompt: *As a journal writer, I want you to promise me that* _____. Ask students to rip the paper out of their notebooks and return to you. On a piece of butcher block paper, write their journal promises. Tape this to a space in your classroom. This will now become the pledge between you and the writer. At least once a month, give them the journal promises for writing consideration. (Always note, students can write their own prompts.)

Celebrate Me (All Grade Levels). Distribute brown lunch bags to each student. Ask them to put their names on the bags. Next to their names, ask students to explain their special backgrounds (family names, specific definitions). If there aren't any, ask students to explain what their names mean to them (in three to five words). Then, ask students to take the bags home and put something special in them (a picture of a loved one, an ingredient to their favorite food, a family keepsake). Every Friday, ask for volunteers to explain and show the contents of their bags. In a respectful and dignified way, students are able to offer a little bit about themselves to their classmates.

Read to Me (All Grade Levels). Choose a day of the week or month to read to your students. It can be a children's classic, such as *Where the Wild Things Are* by Maurice Sendak (1984); or it can be a young adult novel, such as *Divergent* by Veronica Roth (2014); or it can a book of poetry, such as *Inside a Thug's Heart* by Angela Ardis (2004). Ask students to comment in their journals, or ask them to bring in their favorite children's book, young adult novel, or poem. Ask for volunteers to read what they brought to the class. Give your students the gift of fluency by spending quiet time listening or reading.

Cereal and Conversation (All Grade Levels). Nothing says community more than food. Create opportunities for "cooking." How about making a trail mix to enjoy during "Read to Me"? Or how about an afternoon snack of cereal and milk during "Celebrate Me"? Give your students the chance to experience the thoughtful relaxation that good food provides.

Do unto Others (All Grade Levels). What can your students do for others? Can students share their ethnic backgrounds or their family traditions with another class? Could your students read to the elementary school students down the block? Can your students mentor the special education students in their classrooms, becoming their role models? Service to others offers a way for your students to look inward and realize the special gifts they have.

Yoga and Mindfulness (All Grade Levels). Your students are often filled with anxiety due to a number of reasons: family, friends, grades, and so much more. If you are a teacher at a trauma-sensitive school, you often wonder how you can help. Perhaps giving your students specific physical moves or the gift of quiet can assist them in looking inward and resting their brains. Does your district have a mindfulness leader, or is there a nearby yoga teacher who would be willing to work with your group? Whatever support you can offer your students to quiet their anxiety is necessary and essential to their well-being.

It's OK to Laugh (Middle School/High School). Listen to some classic comedy skits or an excerpt from an iconic movie; classic comedy skits include Abbott and Costello's "Who's on First?" or "Lucy Does a TV Commercial" from *I Love Lucy*. Movies include *Ferris Bueller's Day Off*, *The Breakfast Club*, and *Clueless*. Encourage your students to bring in movies, comedy sketches, or jokes that make them laugh. Ask your principal to bring the popcorn and watch some comedy or listen to some jokes with your students. Schedules are tight, and time is at a premium; however, consider giving your class the gift of laughter after a project, unit checkup, or group presentation. Laughter will bring your classroom community even closer together.

Music in Me (All Grade Levels). Ask your students to share their music with the class. Provide time for students to share their music—maybe a piece of music that is important to their family, a piece they have written, or an artist they particularly enjoy. Don't create an assignment from it; don't ask them to analyze it. Enjoy the time to listen to music and reflect.

Your Choice (All Grade Levels). What are some other ways you provide laughter and joy to your students?

CONCLUSION

You have been given a great gift to teach children who need you. While you may feel there are days when you are not appreciated or valued, in truth, your students need you every day to be their family, their friend, and their counselor. You give them the same haven of routine and expectations. They can count on you.

As you create and refine your classroom community, give your students time for both work and play. They deserve it, and so do you. On days when you feel that all is lost, remember this: A simple smile or a high-five from a student can turn your whole day around. Embrace it, and know how much all your students need you.

HOW TO USE CHAPTER 10

Book Study Reflection Question

Provide examples of celebrations in your classroom. Share those with your colleagues.

Professional Learning Community Discussion Question

With your department members, create a "just because" celebration. You deserve it.

Professional Development Discussion Questions

1. As the teacher leader, show your colleagues you appreciate them. Ask them to share celebrations with their colleagues.
2. At the next professional learning community meeting, celebrate those with whom you work. Create a potluck lunch, complete with conversation, music, and laughter!

References

Albert, R. (2017, August 24). A phone call home makes all the difference. *Edutopia*. Retrieved July 8, 2018, from https://www.edutopia.org/article/phone-call-home-makes-all-difference.

Allington, R. L., & Gabriel, R. E. (2012, March). Every child, every day. *Educational Leadership, 69*(6), 10–15.

Ardis, A. (2004). *Inside a thug's heart*. New York: Kensington.

Barati, L. (2015). The impact of eye-contact between teacher and student on L2 learning. *Journal of Applied Linguistics and Language Research, 2*(7), 222–27.

Barnett, T., Lawless, B., Kim, H., & Vista, A. (2017, December 12). Complementary strategies for teaching collaboration and critical thinking skills. *Brookings Institute*. Retrieved July 8, 2018, from https://www.brookings.edu/blog/education-plus-development/2017/12/12/complementary-strategies-for-teaching-collaboration-and-critical-thinking-skills.

Blackburn, B. (2013). *Rigor is NOT a four-letter word*. New York: Routledge.

Brasher, J. (2014). Are gifted children getting lost in the shuffle? *Research News @ Vanderbilt*. Retrieved January 5, 2018, from https://news.vanderbilt.edu/2014/01/06/gifted-children-study.

Buehl, D. (2007). Modeling self-questioning on Bloom's taxonomy. *Wisconsin Education Association Council*. Retrieved July 8, 2018, from http://weac.org/articles/readingroom_modeling.

Cutler, D. (2016, February 26). Strategies for reaching quiet, disengaged, struggling, and troublemaking students. *Edutopia*. Retrieved July 8, 2018, from https://www.edutopia.org/blog/reaching-quiet-disengaged-struggling-troublemaking-students-david-cutler.

DeCostella, K., Byrne, D., & Covington, M. (2013). Unmotivated or motivated to fail? A cross-cultural study of achievement motivation, fear of failure, and student disengagement. *Journal of Educational Psychology*. Retrieved July 8, 2018, from https://openresearch-repository.anu.edu.au/bitstream/1885/14489/2/De%20Castella%20et%20al%20Undermotivated%20or%20Motivated%20to%20Fail%202013.pdf.

Dictionary.com. (n.d.). *Goal*. Retrieved July 8, 2018, from http://www.dictionary.com/browse/goal?s=t.

Dweck, C. S. (2015, January 1). The secret to raising smart kids. *Scientific American*. Retrieved January 3, 2018, from https://www.scientificamerican.com/article/the-secret-to-raising-smart-kids1.

Fisher, D., Frey, N., & Rothenberg, C. (2008). *Content-area conversations: How to plan discussion-based lessons for diverse language learners.* New York: Association for Supervision of Curriculum Development.

Frey, N., & Fisher, D. (2013, January). Close reading. *Principal Leadership, 13*(5), 57–59.

Gilmore, K. (2014, February 14). The Birmingham Children's Crusade of 1963. *Biography.* Retrieved July 8, 2018, from https://www.biography.com/news/black-history-birmingham-childrens-crusade-1963-video.

Golio, G., & Steptoe, J. (2010, October 4). *Jimi: Sounds like a rainbow: A story of the young Jimi Hendrix.* New York: Clarion Books.

Guskey, T. (2011). "Five obstacles to grading reform." *Educational Leadership, (69)*3, 17–21.

Ivey, G. (2011). Opening up the conversation on literacy, college and career. *Journal of Adolescent & Adult Literacy, 55*(2), 96–99.

Jetton, T. L., & Lee, R. (2012). Learning from text: Adolescent literacy from the past decade. In T. L. Jetton & C. Shanahan (Eds.), *Adolescent literacy in the academic disciplines: General principles and practical strategies* (1–32). New York: Guilford Press.

Johnston, P., Ivey, G., & Faulkner, A. (2011). Talking in class: Remembering what is important about classroom talk. *Reading Teacher, 65*(4), 232–37.

Johnston, P. H. (2012). *Opening minds: Using language to change lives.* Portland, ME: Stenhouse.

McKenna, L. (2018, January 5). Will letter grades survive? *Edutopia.* Retrieved July 8, 2018, from https://www.edutopia.org/article/will-letter-grades-survive.

McKibben, S. (2016, September). Parent–teacher conferences: Outdated or underutilized? *ASCD, (58)*9. Retrieved July 8, 2018, from http://www.ascd.org/publications/newsletters/education_update/sept16/vol58/num09/Parent-Teacher_Conferences@_Outdated_or_Un derutilized%C2%A2.aspx.

McLaughlin, C. (2016, September 1). The lasting impact of mispronouncing students' names. *NEA Today.* Retrieved July 8, 2018, from http://neatoday.org/2016/09/01/pronouncing-stu dents-names.

Merriam-Webster. (n.d.). Retrieved July 8, 2018, from https://www.merriam-webster.com.

Platt, R. (2013, November 7). How to take two-column notes. *ASCD Express, 9*(13). Retrieved July 8, 2018, from http://www.ascd.org/ascd-express/vol9/903-video.aspx.

Poe, E. A. (2006). *The best of Poe: The tell-tale heart, the raven, the cask of amontillado, and 30 others.* Smryna, DE: Prestwick House.

Raphael, T., Highfield, K., & Au, K. H. (2006). *QAR now: Question answer relationships (Theory and Practice).* New York: Scholastic.

Roth, V. (2014). *Divergent.* New York: Katherine Tegen Books.

Safir, S. (2016, January 21). Equity vs. equality: 6 steps toward equity. *Edutopia.* Retrieved July 8, 2018, from https://www.edutopia.org/blog/equity-vs-equality-shane-safir.

Salinger, J. D. (1951). *The catcher in the rye.* New York: Little, Brown.

Sendak, M. (1984). *Where the wild things are.* New York: HarperCollins.

Serafini, F. (2011, February). Expanding perspectives for comprehending visual images in multimodal texts. *Journal of Adolescent & Adult Literacy, 54*(5), 342–50. doi:10.1598/JA AL.54.5.4.

Shakespeare, W. (2004). *The Tragedy of Romeo and Juliet.* New York: Simon & Schuster.

Skeeters, K., Campbell, B., Dubitsky, A., Faron, E., Gieselmann, K., George, D., Goldschmidt, B., & Wagner, E. (2016, February). The five reasons we love giving students choice in reading. *English Leadership Quarterly, 38*(3), 6–7. Retrieved July 8, 2018, from http://www.ncte.org/library/NCTEFiles/Resources/Journals/ELQ/0383-feb2016/ELQ0383Top.pdf.

Volavokova, H. (1994). *I never saw another butterfly: Children's drawings and poems from the Terezin concentration camp, 1942–1944.* New York: Schocken.

Wagner, H. (2017, July 17). The science of listening. *Huffington Post.* Retrieved July 8, 2018, from https://www.huffingtonpost.com/heather-wagoner/the-science-of-listening_b_11030950.html.

Whitby, T. (2014, September 17). Educating parents about education. *Edutopia.* Retrieved July 8, 2018, from https://www.edutopia.org/blog/educating-parents-about-education-tom-whitby.

Wisconsin Department of Public Instruction. (2016). Co-teaching in Wisconsin. Retrieved July 8, 2018, from https://dpi.wi.gov/sped/educators/consultation/co-teaching.

Youngs, S. (2012). Injustice and irony: Students respond to Japanese American internment picturebooks. *Journal of Children's Literature, 38*(2), 37–49.

About the Author

Peg Grafwallner, M.Ed., is an instructional coach and reading specialist at a large urban high school in Milwaukee, modeling, coaching, and assisting teachers in creating comprehensive literacy lessons to build skills. As an educator and parent of both a gifted and talented child and a special needs child, Peg advocated for her children's education, explicitly supporting their needs while also reinforcing their teachers' expectations.

www.ingramcontent.com/pod-product-compliance
Lightning Source LLC
Chambersburg PA
CBHW032030230426
43671CB00005B/259